ADVANCE PRAISE FOR

"Teaching Like That"

"Jaime G. A. Grinberg's book provides rich insight into this model institution during its formative stage in the 1930s. Those of us in education schools like to pledge allegiance to the creed of pedagogical progressivism, but the staff of Bank Street in its early days zealously applied these ideas to the practice of teacher preparation, revealing just how rarely our own programs actually do so."

David Labaree, Professor of History of Education, Stanford University, and Vice President, History of Education Division, American Educational Research Association

"Jaime G. A. Grinberg's book is a valuable and long-overdue case study of how cultural, political, and professional forces were negotiated in the early years of Bank Street. Thorough documentation supports his thesis that its initial independence from certain political and bureaucratic forces (being neither a credentialed nor a credentialing institution) allowed Bank Street to pursue a relatively free and open inquiry into teacher education, to develop pedagogical practices informed by that inquiry, and ultimately to construct a distinctive conception of teacher education. Such detailed historical and sociological studies of classrooms, schools and colleges of education that illuminate connections among school experience, gender, social class, and community issues are scarce in the literature. Grinberg's discoveries have important implications for contemporary educational administration, educational policy, and teacher education, particularly within the progressive tradition."

Maughn Gregory, Director, Institute for the Advancement of Philosophy for Children, and Associate Professor of Educational Foundations, Montclair State University

"Teaching Like That"

Studies in the Postmodern Theory of Education

Joe L. Kincheloe and Shirley R. Steinberg
General Editors

Vol. 234

PETER LANG
New York • Washington, D.C./Baltimore • Bern
Frankfurt am Main • Berlin • Brussels • Vienna • Oxford

Jaime G. A. Grinberg

"Teaching Like That"

The Beginnings of Teacher Education at Bank Street

PETER LANG

New York • Washington, D.C./Baltimore • Bern
Frankfurt am Main • Berlin • Brussels • Vienna • Oxford

Library of Congress Cataloging-in-Publication Data

Grinberg, Jaime G. A.
"Teaching like that": the beginnings of teacher education at Bank Street /
Jaime G. A. Grinberg.
p. cm. — (Counterpoints: studies in the postmodern theory
of education; 234)
Includes bibliographical references.
1. Student teachers—Training of—United States. 2. Progressive education.
3. Bank Street College of Education—History. I. Title.
II. Series: Counterpoints (New York, N.Y.) 234.
LB2157.U5G75   370'.71—dc22   2004027486
ISBN 0-8204-6239-X
ISSN 1058-1634

Bibliographic information published by **Die Deutsche Bibliothek**.
Die Deutsche Bibliothek lists this publication in the "Deutsche
Nationalbibliografie"; detailed bibliographic data is available
on the Internet at http://dnb.ddb.de/.

Cover design by Joni Holst

The paper in this book meets the guidelines for permanence and durability
of the Committee on Production Guidelines for Book Longevity
of the Council of Library Resources.

To Hannah, Mihal, and Binyamin
To Katia

Contents

List of Figures

Acknowledgments

I am thankful to Joe Kincheloe and Shirley Steinberg for their support, trust, understanding, caring, respect, intellectual stimulation, time, challenge, help, and interest in my work.

A number of people, teachers and friends, have been supportive, helpful, and intellectually stimulating in relation to this project. Each one of them provided a unique and meaningful way of nurturing. Their questions, their suggestions, their guidance, and our conversations were invaluable. They are David Labaree, Bill McDiarmid, Sharon Feiman-Nemser, Helen Featherstone, Jay Featherstone, Jeremy Price, Michelle Parker, Kathryn Herr, Gary Anderson, Elizabeth Saavedra, Monica Pini, Gustavo Fischman, Susan Katz, Linda Ware, Debbie Harris, Constanza Hazelwood, and Margery Osborne. I am also thankful to my colleagues in the department of Educational Foundations at Montclair State University for their encouragement. They organized a series of colloquiums at the Institute for the Advancement of Philosophy for Children for me to present and discuss my work. Their feedback and suggestions were very important. Many thanks to Maughn Gregory, David Kennedy, Megan Laverty, Ann Sharp, Tamara Lucas, Jacqui Mosselson, Alina Reznitskaya, Mark Weinstein, George Bernstein, and Mathew Lippman.

I am thankful to the teachers and students at Bank Street in the 1930s that took the risk and created a wonderful unique space. Their stories and experiences, their thinking, passion, and practices made the world of many children a better place.

My daughters Hannah and Mihal and my son Binyamin help me to keep life in perspective and to set my priorities right. Their love is unconditional, their humor is inspiring, their thoughtfulness is engaging and challenging, their patience and tolerance are unique, and their love is my strength. Their experiences in schools, their thinking about classrooms, teachers, and learning, have inspired me to keep searching. My wife Katia Paz Goldfarb is not only a great partner, but also an incredible scholar. She supported and stimulated my thinking. She read several drafts, challenged my assumptions, and asked excellent questions. Many great suggestions she provided made the book better. Her love and understanding made my work possible. Words cannot capture my grateful feelings.

I am also thankful to Montclair State University for enabling me to receive a faculty scholarship incentive to carry on with the writing of this book.

The folks at Peter Lang have been very helpful with the production process and the editing. I am grateful for their work, particularly to Bernadette Shade.

I appreciate permission to adapt for this book part of an article I authored that was published by Teachers College Record:
"I had never been exposed to teaching like that": Progressive teacher education at Bank Street during the 1930's. *Teachers College Record*, 104 (7), 1422-1460.

Certainly, the responsibility is mine, including the errors.

Preface

By Joe L. Kincheloe

If you have not discovered the scholarship of Jaime Grinberg, this volume will serve as an introduction to the work of one of the world's top scholars in critical and progressive education. Grinberg is an impassioned scholar whose humanity and dedication to the life of the mind, issues of justice, and rigorous scholarship shows up on every page of his books, chapters, and articles. He is a treasured resource for those of us operating in the critical pedagogical domain. I know that when I don't know or can't remember a particular researcher's name or, more importantly, when I need an interpretation of a particular text or socio-political situation that I can count on Jaime to come up with a compelling insight that I had not previously considered. When such genius is combined with Grinberg's generosity and humility, we are blessed with a special presence in the world. Jaime Grinberg is indeed a special presence who operates to make the world a better place for all who are lucky enough to come into contact with him.

In this history of Bank Street's teacher education program, Grinberg exhibits his historiographical and hermeneutic skills. Understanding the importance of the ideas that Lucy Sprague Mitchell and many, many others brought to school, Jaime documents the power of their ideas and the pedagogy they implemented. As I read the book, I was struck with the vast number of concepts promoted in the program that are still viewed as innovative and even radical today. Grinberg teases these ideas out of the historical record and provides them to us for consideration as twenty-first century readers. Consider just a few of these progressive concepts. The program's concern with

- Social justice as exemplified not only in the classroom curriculum but in field trips to coal mines in Pennsylvania and West Virginia.
- The socio-political forces that shape the lives of students and construct their relationship to teaching and learning.
- The development of problem-based curricula.

- Innovations in cognition based on relational types of thinking.
- The employment of a sophisticated, Deweyan experiential education grounded on questioning and interpreting experience in ways that informed future action.
- The necessity for teachers to learn about the self, world, students, and schooling and their interrelationships in their effort to become rigorous, inspirational educators.
- The importance of educating teachers as scholars, writers, and curriculum constructors.
- The nature of "mind" and how students learn—the ways they construct meaning in relation to their environments.
- The transformative nature of pedagogy.
- The education of teachers who understand the learning process and can apply such insight to their roles as curriculum developers.
- The power of site-based teacher education—the importance of professional education students learning to teach in the context of the everyday life in schools.

These, of course, are just a few of the concepts that Grinberg addresses in his history of teacher education at Bank Street. Such a list gives readers insight into the contemporary importance of what Grinberg has produced here. Of course, it is a history that will be interesting to scholars on a variety of levels, but it is also a book with great import for contemporary teacher education. In the coming years the importance of Jaime Grinberg's contribution to contemporary educational scholarship will become apparent to more and more students of pedagogy. This book merely whets our appetite for what is yet to come from this special presence in our field. I am proud to write the preface for this book and to work with Jaime on his numerous scholarly projects. His vision of what teacher education and pedagogy can become serves as an inspiration to those of us committed to a just, progressive, and empowering education in the darkness of this neo-colonialist, regressive era.

CHAPTER ONE

Introduction

> This was the most exciting thing that ever happened to me: To take those courses with those women. I had never been exposed to teaching like that.
>
> Beyer, 9/29/78, p. 3

This book is the story of the first years of the teacher education program of the Cooperative School for Student Teachers. Years later it became the Bank Street College of Education. The name Bank Street comes from the daily use by the participants of its programs referring to the street were the cooperative was located together with other programs and a nursery school at 69 Bank Street, New York, in the midst of the Village. The focus of this book are the practices that a group of students and teachers experienced in this progressive teacher education program during the 1930s, when the program started and was independent of state norms and of school and academic conventions. The purpose of this book is to provide examples, describe, and analyze the characteristics of teaching prospective teachers in a progressive teacher education institution which had a primary emphasis on early childhood and early elementary education. Thus, this book will primarily address what the Bank Street teacher education program was about and what it was like to be at Bank Street's teacher preparation program during its beginning years. In short, this book will look into "teaching like that," its meaning, its characteristics, its conceptual grounding.

The evidence provided in this book will show that this program represented a distinctive conception of what a teacher should experience. These experiences fostered the type of teaching that the institution hoped its graduates would enact when teaching children, with a strong orientation to making the teaching processes a subject matter of study. This means that at the center of these structured experiences were the teacher and the learner engaging as inquirers. Nowadays there are important and sophisticated arguments and practices that engage in student and teacher inquiry, but at the time it was a novelty since teachers were not prepared to teach progressively by developing the habit of inquiry (for contemporary practices of student and teacher inquiry in teacher education; see, for example, Steinberg and Kincheloe, 1998; Kincheloe 2002; Splitter & Sharp, 1995).

The case of Bank Street will present the reader with a radical alternative in terms of institutional culture, conceptual approaches, ways of knowing, ways of teaching, and ways of relating and building relationships, in contrast to the dominant nature of teacher education programs in the past and in many aspects of the present. This program during this special historical time, which also encompassed the early years of its foundation, fostered a commitment to social change which started in the classroom, but permeated the students and faculty disposition toward life. Furthermore, the early years of Bank Street help us imagine possibilities and think differently from the mainstream dominant discourses of teacher education reform that privilege cause-effect relationships of teaching on learning measured in standardized tests. Learning from the case of the early years of Bank Street provides an opportunity to depart from the enslaving chains featured by schools and colleges of education and arts and sciences. These kinds of school have often reproduced a glorification of mediocre anti-intellectualism that silences and docilizes future teachers, socializing and domesticating them to fit into school systems that perpetuate inequity, discrimination, alienation, and poor academics. Paradoxically, these are the very same schools that need to be reclaimed away from entrenched bureaucrats who, perhaps unintentionally, sustain and nurture institutional violence toward teachers, students, and themselves often by accepting what Hannah Arendt labeled the banality of evil. Programs that prepare teachers are notorious in general for their jealousy prioritizing methodologically reductionist practices away from intellectual inquiry, systematic data collection, and critical thinking. These issues have been well discussed in the literature on teacher education as in, among many others, Ginsburg, 1988, Liston & Zeichner, 1990, Grinberg & Goldfarb, 1998, Popkewitz, 1987, Zeichner et al, 1998, Grinberg & Saavedra, 2000, Zeichner, 2003, or Kincheloe, 2004.

I am not claiming the case of the early years of Bank Street as a model for contemporary teacher education. Particularly it is a problematic model since it was in many ways, as it will be discussed in this book, a privileged institution, preparing privileged students, to the extent that women were privileged and had power in the 1930s, to teach in most cases in privileged private experimental progressive schools (Antler, 1997; Gordon, 1988; Grinberg, 2001, 2002). Certainly, given these women's commitment to social justice and their awareness about their privilege, they aimed at moving from the private environments into the public realm, working with and influencing directions and practices in public schools (Grinberg, 2001). In spite of not searching for a model, it is this book's intention to highlight unique, distinctive approaches that could be relevant to many aspects of contemporary teacher education change. Their alternative thinking, their alternative practices, their commitments to critical inquiry not only into school matters but also into their own selves and into their social, economic, and political contexts, their commitment to talk to power and exercise power to benefit their students, themselves, and the multiple communities where they acted as well as society at large, present the reader with interesting and relevant opportunities to open a space for hope. This case presents a regime of truth drastically alternative to the dominant regimes (for a discussion of regimes of truth vis-à-vis education, which is a framework of analysis discussed in the work of the French scholar M. Foucault, 1981, 1990; see for example Anderson & Grinberg, 1998; Gore, 1993; Popkewitz, 1987; or Segall, 2002).

Purposely this book will neither cover contemporary teacher education reform, nor it will articulate a proposal for change. I prefer to present the story and to provide an opportunity to listen to the oral histories that compose an important source of information for this book. I let the readers draw their own connections as I see a difference between the researcher/story teller and that of the policy maker or teacher educator. I will tell you the story as I organized it, as I digested it and as I made sense of it. I made sense of it by looking at teacher education through the lenses of pedagogical practices. Looking closely to the routines of learning to teach in concrete and contingent historical and educational spaces enables an understanding of a dimension that cannot be legislated in the education of practitioners: the meaning of experiences constituted by interactions and relationships. This is relevant particularly for the preparation of progressive teachers, many of whom never experienced progressive teaching. This book will explore and unpack these concepts within the context of Bank Street and it will show that it was possible to have a highly intellectual and inquiry oriented teacher education program, with a rigorous study of "experience," with a passion to understand children, subject matter, social contexts, and the self, and with a commitment to justice (for a description of data sources and methodological approach see Appendix A).

Bank Street College of Education

Bank Street College of Education was privately established in 1930 by a group of directors of experimental schools in need of progressive teachers. These directors approached Lucy Sprague Mitchell, who directed the Bureau of Educational Experiments, a private research organization, and who also co-founded an experimental nursery school (Antler, 1982; Gordon, 1988). Bank Street is a very unique case of teacher education because it existed as a private organization where some of the disabling elements identified by the literature on the history of teacher preparation were not present (the reader should note that throughout this book the names Bank Street, Bank Street College of Education, and Cooperative School, Cooperative School for Teachers, or Cooperative School for Student Teachers, CST or CSST, will be used alternatively and refer to the same institution and to the same teacher education program). For instance, issues of market pressures, social status, and class and gender, are different at Bank Street because of the social class background, and cultural capital, of both the students and instructors in the program, who were mostly women educated in prestigious private liberal arts colleges (Bourdieau, 1977, argued that cultural capital can be defined as "instruments for the appropriation of symbolic wealth socially designed as worthy of being sought and possessed," p. 488).

This institution was independent of any school district or university, thus freeing it from many political and hierarchical conflicts, and from bureaucratic processes to carry on changes and innovations (Labaree, 1993; Urban, 1990; Warren, 1985). Its faculty did not have an academic background in terms of traditional scholarship (although some did); they were not the traditional professor living within the rules and rights of universities, and their commitment and focus was on the teacher preparation program; different from many universities and normal schools (Herbst, 1989). Also, its students were different from students in other teacher education programs in universities and/or normal schools and did not provide a credential or a degree for several years.

Lucy Sprague Mitchell was the key faculty member and the main force behind the organization (Antler, 1987). She was educated at elite places, as were most of the faculty—in particular Smith College, and also Radcliff, Columbia, Chicago, and some European institutions. The faculty represented a variety of disciplinary backgrounds and expertise. However, as it will be described in this book, most of them were educated at the same or similar places. This is an important issue to consider because almost all of the students also were educated at these same types of institutions. This suggests that there is a connection of a strong common culture of shared experiences; similar liberal education, similar places, similar professors, similar social class background, similar friends, similar values, and similar expectations.

These shared cultural and educational experiences influenced the ways in which the curriculum at Bank Street was organized and the kind of pedagogical practices fostered in the program. This connection also shaped the recruiting and admission processes. Bank Street sought students who differed from the typical student in normal schools and in other teacher education programs. The CST wanted students with academic experience and life experience. Most students in the beginning years (1931-1936) were women who graduated from elite liberal arts colleges such as Wellesley, Smith, Reed, or Radcliff. This is a rather different class background from the reported background of students in most Normal Schools. This information is congruent with what Semel (Sadovnik & Semel, 1992) discusses as "the paradox" of progressive education, which refers to what could be an important contradiction between commitments to social justice and democracy and the fact that they mostly taught in private elite and middle-class schools. However, on the other hand, it has been an explicit commitment of Lucy Sprague Mitchell to move their work into public schools. Sprague Mitchell documented that work in her book "Our children, our schools" (1950) and Antler (1987) also documented this evidence.

Moreover, because Bank Street was not part of a university, it was free of the competing pressures over student credit hours with colleges of arts and sciences. Furthermore, different from many other teacher education programs the faculty that taught in the program had ownership over it. Another difference was the fact that during the early 1930s, the program did not provide a New York State teaching license, which means that they were free to establish their own curriculum without having to conform to outside standards. This last point is an important characteristic of the first few years because they were not "regulated" by the state. However, in a sense the school members of the cooperative regulated them. At any rate, whether the state, the profession, and/or the markets, are regulating there is some form of external control always present. Thus, the questions over teacher education regulations are connected with power arrangements since the mechanisms of control such as standards, tests, and/or markets are not free from these processes.

This topic is interesting because it has been "silent" in both, the dominant historical literature about the history of teacher education and in the dominant literature about progressivism. By silent I mean that Bank Street has not been treated or mentioned as influential or relevant by influential scholars who wrote about the history of teacher education or the history of progressivism (for instance, see Church & Sedlak, 1976; Clifford & Guthrie, 1988; Cremin, 1961; Cuban, 1993; Ginsburg, 1988; Goodlad et al., 1990; Herbst, 1989; Kliebard, 1995; Labaree, 1994; Urban, 1990; Warren, 1985). In the dominant narratives about the history of progressive education, Bank Street and its faculty or students are rarely mentioned. For example, in the influential work about progressive education by Cremin (1964), Bank Street or its faculty are mentioned two times in the main text, one time in reference to artist-teachers (p. 206), and one time in reference to some tensions among progressive educators (p. 289). They are also mentioned in the same work one time in a footnote (p. 204n), and one time in the bibliographical notes (p. 377). Comparing with other schools, people, and ideas, in the same volume, Bank Street is not a central player. This "silence" could be explained based on an array of combined reasons. For instance, it could be that Bank Street was small in size; its focus was on the education of young children; most of the instructors were not Ph.D.s but rather came from a very practice oriented background; the vast majority of the participants were women; many of the students and teachers in the program were from an elite social class background; it was a private institution, and the program was a very unique and different case which was very difficult to fit and explain.

The study of the experiences at Bank Street provides a case to illustrate what Clifford (1980) pointed as missing in the literature: "...the pronounced disposition to place educational history in the context of impersonal social forces and such mass movements as modernization, bureaucratization, and professionalization further diminishes the persons whose experiences is the stuff of history" (p. 143). Furthermore, in this same essay she suggested:

> There are no histories of classrooms, of which I am aware, and
> school and college histories (institutional histories) say virtually
> nothing in a systematic and analytical way about life in schools, or

about the range of interactions of school experience, with ethnicity, gender, social class, or community. (p. 144)

There is a need for thorough descriptions or accounts of how some structural changes in education were actually experienced and negotiated in specific contexts by particular individuals. Reinforcing this view that calls for research that describe and analyze practices and meanings in historical events, Finkelstein (1992) contends that

Focusing on the analysis of structure rather than process, prescription rather than practice, and ideology rather than consciousness, historians of education had unknowingly concealed private processes from view (e.g., the formation and evolution of community, the acquisition of identity, the cultivation of intellect, sensibility, and aspiration). (p. 284)

Last, but not least, I had an extraordinary interest in the theme because of my own background as a teacher in experimental alternative public education who always heard good things about Bank Street College of Education from friends, colleagues, relatives, and teachers of mine, and also because of being a parent of young children in school age. The "ethos" among practitioners about the virtues of this institution is not of little accomplishment since most of what I learned and heard about Bank Street was from teachers' word of mouth, not only in the United States, but also in South America. The study about Bank Street served as an avenue to explore my interest in connecting my own preoccupation and struggles with radically changing teacher education and with my commitment of seeing education as a possibility to advance social transformations by fostering critical pedagogies and democratic and just organizations.

As Clifford (1980) reminds us, "A given piece of historical research often provides glimpses into the particular worries of the historian's own times...Audience or readership reaction to historical research is also a gauge of the temper of the times" (p. 155). As an educator with a strong commitment to radically change, not just reform, the ways in which teachers are prepared, exploring the beginnings of an alternative program for the teaching of teachers at Bank Street seemed a fascinating adventure. Thus, this book provides a space for the voices of the participants and their stories in connection with their learning to teach, and it will go inside the classroom and look closely at practices that are framed as progressive.

According to Antler (1987), Bank Street attempted to provide a synthesis among some of the contemporary progressive perspectives of the 1930s. She argues that "During the Depression, the search for a redefinition of the relationship between individuals and society brought fresh support to progressive educators who believed that the classroom could become the model for a new collectivism, integrating self-expression with larger social goals" (Antler, 1987, p. 307). As a program, Bank Street shows the blending of these perspectives in a coherent manner within the institution's curriculum and teaching of prospective teachers and in relation to the sites where student teachers practiced, with attention to a radical critique of society and with interest in child-centered practices.

The focus of the time, the 1930s, is a result of several reasons. First, during these years, the teacher education program was not subjected to State regulations for licensure. Second, the program was formed in 1930, and it is interesting to see how the participants shaped the early experiences, which established some of the traditions on which Bank Street rests. Third, the data that refers to the teaching itself is in one way or another present for these years, in particular through a set of oral histories, which is more limited for the following years. Also, the 1930s were times with heavy ideological discussion (Tyack, Lowe, & Hansot, 1984). Moreover, these authors argue that:

> The rise of totalitarianism was making Americans newly conscious of the importance of democratic beliefs and processes, and there was lively debate among educators about how to relate schools to the larger society and economy. It was an era of aggressive professionalism in education, when standards for certification and education of teachers and specialists were rising in a buyers' labor market. But one could also argue that hard times were not propitious for innovation, that school people had such trouble merely maintaining earlier gains that they had little opportunity to experiment, and that what school boards and other power-wielders in local communities wanted was not advanced ideologies but the old verities, not fads and frills but the basics. (p. 143)

Bank Street emphasized that teachers must understand and enjoy children, but teachers should know the world in which children live and understand the social, political, and economic contexts which condition the environment in which children grow up and develop. This assumes a need for the teacher's own social perspectives to be explored and the need for teachers to engage actively as participants in social and civic responsibilities. At Bank Street this meant that teachers should be active in the shaping of a nurturing and just society for the healthy growth and needs of children as well as adults. This necessary disposition and knowledge for teaching comes from the perspective that there is a need not only for inquiring and understanding, but also for engaging and shaping the contemporary social conditions through teaching and other activities.

> [There is] Evidence that the experiences which determine the educational development of the child are not confined to the school but relate equally to the whole amount of experiences outside the school --in the home and elsewhere-- by which humans beings undertake to satisfy their basic needs for food, clothes, houses, health, economic security, satisfying social relations, recreation, and creative expression.
>
> Outline, 1937, pp. 3-4

This type of disposition also embraces an experimental propensity and a constant reflective and critical attitude. In 1931 Lucy Sprague Mitchell wrote in the journal "Progressive Education" that:

> To promote the development of personal powers, we propose to treat the student-teachers as we should treat children-only on a higher age level. We propose to give them a program of 'experiences' in exploring their local environment which will sensitize them to this environment, quicken their powers of observation, enlarge their "intake" by making more active their senses and their motor life. The study of the environment, as we plan it, will be based upon fieldwork. We hope our students will explore, not only the geographic world in which they live, but also the cultural and social-economic world. (Pp. 252-253)

Organization of the Book

This introductory chapter has explained the purpose of this book and briefly described some aspects of the early years of Bank Street, as well as discussed reasons and motivations for this book. Chapter 2 describes the creation of the program, its beginnings, and the people and institutional membership. In Chapter 3 the focus shifts to discuss the curricular organization of the program and the dimensions of learning to teach. Chapter 4 provides detailed accounts of the teaching of 2 classes taught by Lucy Sprague Mitchell, and provides information about teaching in other classes as well. Chapter 5 analyzes the characteristics of "teaching like that." Chapter 6 explores the conceptual grounds for this program at Bank Street during its early years as well as some conceptual programmatic aspects of it. Chapter 7 describes the organizational structure of the institution, its financial situation, and the students' recruiting and selection procedures. Chapter 8 locates this program vis-à-vis progressive education and chapter 9 looks at the impact of the program using documents from students' evaluations and from schools' hiring agents in addition to a description of the market for the program graduates. Chapter 10, the conclusion, summarizes the main arguments presented in this book.

CHAPTER TWO

The Cooperative School for Student Teachers

The teacher education program created by the Bureau of Educational Experiments in 1930 in New York was called The Cooperative School for Student Teachers (CST). Because its new building was located in 69 Bank Street, the institution was informally called by the name of the street. The Bank Street program in the 1930s was independent of most of the factors that shaped other teacher education programs. The program focused on preparing teachers for progressive and experimental schools. The Cooperative School for Teachers offered an intensive one-year, professional teacher education curriculum for college graduates who were mostly interested in teaching young and elementary school age children (two to thirteen years of age, which includes middle school nowadays). The following statement captures the essence of the CST educational approach:

> Our aim is to help students develop a scientific attitude towards their work and towards life. To use this means an attitude of eager, alert observations; a constant questioning of old procedures in the light of new observations; ...an effort to keep as reliable records as the situation permits in order to base the future upon actual knowledge of the experience of the past.
>
> Our aim is equally to help students develop and express the attitude of the artist towards their work and towards life. To us this means an attitude of relish, of emotional drive, a genuine participation in some creative phase of work, and a sense that joy and beauty are legitimate possessions of all human beings, young and old. We are not interested in perpetuating any 'school of thought.' Rather, we are interested in imbuing teachers with an experimental, critical and ardent approach to their work.
>
> Sprague Mitchell, 1931, p. 251.

This chapter will describe how the program began, how it came to be, and its institutional arrangements during the 1930s. In addition, this chapter will explore the students and faculty, the cooperating schools, the admission processes, and will introduce the program curriculum.

Meeting a Need

The Cooperative School started to organize in 1930 as a joint effort of the Bureau for Educational Experiments (BEE) and a group of progressive private schools. The Bureau was created and directed by Lucy Sprague Mitchell in 1916. Its purpose was to do research on childhood and on education. Most studies were done in experimental nursery schools. The Bureau had its own nursery school which functioned at the Mitchells' house (Antler, 1982). Edith Gordon (1988) reports that in 1929 several meetings took place at the BEE library between leaders of private progressive schools 'to discuss their mutual interests and problems' (p. 205).

Needing to prepare teachers for their schools, a group of private progressive schools approached Lucy Sprague Mitchell asking for help. Mitchell had had experience with professional development through her work with Caroline Pratt at the City and Country School where teachers had some activities like map making or block playing, which aimed at enhancing their understanding of children, learning, systematic inquiry, and classroom life (Winsor, 2/24/75).

The purpose was to prepare teachers to teach in progressive experimental schools. In her book on experimental schools, Charlotte Winsor (1973) refers to them as schools that fostered a scientific approach to their practices. According to Winsor, these schools kept careful records of their activities and of children's changes, learning, and growth. The purpose was to identify effective ways of nurturing children's growth. These schools were systematic in their observations, record keeping, and analysis. The BEE was very helpful collecting data and analyzing patterns. The schools curriculum focused on children and practices were progressive. In spite of it, according to the reports of the Bureau in Winsor's book, practices and curriculum drew on different perspectives, like psychoanalysis, and they varied from place to place. The influence of the directors shaped the direction of the school life. Among the schools mentioned as progressive and experimental were Walden School, City and Country School, The Ethical Culture School, and the

Nursery School, which was the school located in the Mitchells' house and that years later became the school of Bank Street.

Traditional teacher preparation programs did not prepare the type of teachers these schools needed. Further, Caroline Pratt, the director of the progressive City and Country School, which had a history of association with the Bureau of Educational Experiments, stated that she preferred to hire teachers without teacher training programs rather than hire teachers with such preparation (Winsor, 2/24/75). She thought that such preparation narrowed teachers' minds so that they needed to be retrained.

According to progressive educators, Normal Schools and universities did a poor job preparing teachers. The critiques centered on the overwhelming emphasis that conventional or mainstream teacher education programs gave to methods and the limited attention paid to children, child development, and the social context of childhood and schooling.

> Certainly, the normal schools and teachers college, with an occasional conspicuous exception, are not sending out the teachers that are needed, though they may eventually do a better job if they can ever extricate themselves from the 'principles of education,' methods courses, and other impedimenta that clutter up the educational baggage-car.
>
> Editorial, 1931, p. 280.

The Cooperative School for Student Teachers, a teacher education program, resulted from a need to supply teachers for private progressive and experimental schools who could foster, continue, and enhance their practices and philosophies.

> As a result of the teacher-training situation, progressive schools have been hard put to it to get the kind of teachers they must have. One finds Shady Hill and Beaver County Day School working out an apprenticeship system of their own, not because this is necessarily the ideal way, but because of urgent necessity, and eight schools in the New York region joining with the Bureau of Educational Experiments in organizing a cooperative school for student teachers.
>
> Editorial, 1931, p. 280.

The Cooperative School, then, was grounded in the ideas about teaching and schooling fostered and advanced by the experimental schools within the progressive perspective. The first cohort of students (22) started the program during the 1931-1932 academic year. A research report published in *Progressive Education*, by Frederick G. Bonner (1929, p. 111), which in a survey identified progressive teaching characteristics, summarizes the following:

> From these statements of teachers and directors of progressive schools there emerge certain well-defined, inclusive teacher qualifications that are outstanding and significant. These elements of the teachers' preparation may be placed under five closely related heads. In general terms, the teacher-training institution should develop in teachers:
> 1. Scholarship or cultural background.
> 2. A progressive conception of education
> 3. An inquiring, creative, constructive, open-minded attitude.
> 4. An understanding of the behavior, means of growth and needs of children.
> 5. Training in the techniques of teaching under efficient, progressive guidance.

The implication is that to be able to teach in progressive schools, prospective teachers had to be prepared within the progressive perspective. Furthermore, as will be shown in the next chapters, the Bank Street program also fostered a preparation that provided the student of teaching with the opportunity to experience progressive teaching not just during practice-teaching, but also exposed and engaged them as students to such teaching by their teacher educators.

The Cooperating Schools

The CST and progressive schools in the area were intimately connected. The teacher education program was created because of a need to staff these schools with teachers trained within this educational perspective. Students were placed in these schools for practice teaching. Furthermore, many CST graduates got teaching jobs at these schools.

The following is a list of the cooperating schools in 1934-1935 with a brief description of them (Annual Report, 1934-1935). Many Bank Street students lived in these schools during the week until Thursdays when they went to Bank Street for classes.

1. Carson College for Orphan Girls, Flourtown, Pa, was a boarding school. Elsa Ueland, was the President. This institution provided school and home life in a country setting for orphan girls from age six through age eighteen. This place served mostly students who already completed their year at Bank Street and who were seeking a second year with more specialization. Bank Street students were provided with full maintenance but commuting expenses.

2. Little Red School House, 196 Bleeker Street, New York. Elizabeth Irwin was the Director. This day school still exists today. It started as a continuation of co-educational experimental classes that were conducted in Public School 41, New York, by a group of educators and parents affiliated with the Progressive Education Association. The school taught children from age five through age eleven and a few years later through age thirteen in order to cover the range of K-8 grades. Up to three Bank Street students were provided with room, lunches, and use of the kitchen.

3. Mount Kemble School, Morristown, New Jersey. Helen Garrett was the Director. It was a co-educational country day school. The students ranged from three years old to twelve years old. This school provided room, lunches, and use of kitchen in addition to commuting expenses for three Bank Street students.

4. Nursery School, Bureau of Educational Experiments, 69 Bank Street, New York, was the lab school of the institution that still exists. Harriet M. Johnson and Jessie Stanton were the Directors. It was a co-educational full-day school with children from two to five years old. It provided lunches at cost for the student-teachers. It became the Harriet Johnson Nursery School when she passed away in 1935.

5. Rosemary Junior School, Greenwich, Connecticut. Ellen Steele was the Director of this suburban day school. The school was co-educational up to age six, with girls in older classes up to the age of twelve. This school provided lunches for Bank Street students, offered a few partial scholarships to attend CST, and helped organize living arrangements for the student-teachers.

6. Spring Hill School, Litchfield, Connecticut. Mabel Spinney and Dorothy Bull were the school Principals of this co-educational country day and boarding school. The children ranged from age six through twelve. The school provided a full maintenance to Bank

Street students, except for commuting expenses. Mostly second-year students who wanted extra experiences were placed in this school.

7. Woodward School, 321 Clinton Avenue, Brooklyn, N. Y. The Director was E. Frances Woodward. It was a co-educational day school for children from age four through age fourteen. Bank Street students were placed especially in older age groups. Lunches were provided to the student-teachers, and the school assisted in making inexpensive living arrangements for them.

The relationship with the cooperating schools was very close. The directors of the cooperating schools had weekly meetings with the rest of the faculty at Bank Street since they were members of the planning committee of the Cooperative School. Among other issues, student progress was discussed in these meetings. Furthermore, on different occasions, some directors and some teachers from the cooperating schools taught courses at Bank Street. The CST stressed a coherent and coordinated effort by having, first, a small number of cooperating schools that shared a vision about teaching from a progressive perspective. Second, by having a small number of student teachers. Third, they stressed such coordination by having a close working cooperation with teachers and schools. Coherence and coordination facilitated this crucial aspect of learning to teach: the practice-teaching experience.

Faculty Members

Lucy Sprague Mitchell, the key faculty member and the main force behind the organization was educated at elite places, as were most of the faculty members. Following there is a list and a brief description of faculty who taught in the program during the 1933-1934 year, based on the "CST Catalogue" (1933-1934) and on the "Petition for Replacement of Provisional Charter" (1940).

1. Barbara Biber, a psychologist, taught courses in child development. She attended the University of Chicago and Columbia University, where she got her doctorate, and worked with the psychiatrist, Herman Adler, in the Institute of Juvenile Research. Biber directed a study of children's drawing at the Bureau (BEE). Through the years she gained an international

reputation as central researcher and thinker on child development and education. Her books and articles were translated into several languages.

2. Marion Farquhar, the music instructor, was a personal friend of Lucy Sprague Mitchell. She studied music with famous musicians in New York, Boston, and Paris, and she was very well connected with the musical community. As a result, she invited Pablo Casals to teach some music lessons at Bank Street while he was a visiting conductor of the New York Philharmonic Orchestra.

3. Elizabeth Healy, the General Secretary of the CST, taught the class on the development of personality. She was a psychiatric social worker with the Philadelphia Child Guidance Clinic. She studied at the University of Minnesota and at Smith College.

4. Elisabeth Irwin was the director of Little Red School House, one of the cooperating schools. She taught several classes connected with curriculum. She was also a journalist, and her contributions were published in professional and non-professional journals. She studied at Smith College, at Columbia University, and at the New York School of Social Work.

5. Harriet Johnson organized the Nursery School at Bank Street and served as its director since 1919 when the institution was the Bureau of Educational Experiments. She taught the classes on observation and record keeping. Before becoming a teacher she was a nurse and was involved in psychological work. Johnson also worked with the New York Public Schools. She published several books on young children, nursery schools, and block building. There is no information available about her formal education.

6. Polly Korchien, a close friend of Lucy Sprague Mitchell, taught dance at the CST. She studied dance in Germany at the Pupil Wigman School and was connected with several dance circles in New York, including students of Martha Graham and Isadora Duncan.

7. Clara Lambert was an assistant to Lucy Sprague Mitchell in the courses on Environment and Map Making. She co-authored some work with Lucy Sprague Mitchell. Lambert studied at the

University of Minnesota and at Columbia University. She was also active in the Women's Section of the Republican party.

8. Lucy Sprague Mitchell was the founder and organizer of the Bureau of Educational Experiments and of what became Bank Street. She was also a Board member, Chair of the Working Council, and Chair of the Central Staff. Mitchell studied at Radcliffe College. She taught at the University of California, Berkeley, where she was the first Dean of Women before moving to New York. Mitchell taught several courses in the CST. She published several articles and books for professional audiences and several books for children and for teachers.

9. Ralph Pearson, a renowned artist, taught at the New School for Social research. He taught the Design Workshop at CST. He had several exhibitions and was known as a leader of the "modern" movement in art.

10. Charlotte Perry, a teacher at Rosemary Junior School, one of the cooperating schools, was a member of the first cohort of students at the CST. She studied at Smith College, at the Art Institute, Chicago, at the Ann Morgan Dramatic School and at the Moscow Art Theater. She also studied at the New York School of Social Work and was involved with the Association House Settlement. Perry taught dramatics at the CST.

11. Jessie Stanton was a co-director of the Nursery School at Bank Street. She was an experienced teacher who developed several techniques for classroom research and curriculum assessment focusing on the child. Stanton taught curriculum classes at the CST and wrote several book chapters and books on children's play and on literacy.

12. Ellen Steele was the director of Rosemary Junior School, a cooperating school with the CST. She studied at Teachers College, Columbia University and taught at many progressive schools. Steele published articles in "Progressive Education" on the progressive school teacher and on art and dramatics. She taught curriculum classes at the CST.

These faculty members represented a variety of backgrounds and expertise. Most of them were educated at the same or similar places. This is an important issue to consider because as we will see in the section on the students' background that many of them also were educated at these institutions. This suggests that there is a connection of a strong common culture of shared experience: a similar liberal education, similar places, similar professors, similar social class background, similar friends, similar values, and similar expectations. These shared cultural and educational experiences influenced the ways in which the curriculum at Bank Street was organized and the kind of pedagogical practices fostered in the program. This connection also shaped the recruiting and admission processes, which are discussed in chapter seven.

Students

Bank Street sought students who differed from the typical student in Normal schools and in other teacher education programs. Most students in standard teacher education programs were females from low middle-class and working-class background (Ginsburg, 1987; Rury, 1989). Also, most of these students in traditional teacher education programs had a poor academic background, and they were undergraduate students (Goodlad et al., 1990; Herbst, 1989; Labaree, 1993; Rury, 1989). The CST wanted students with academic experience and life experience. Most students in the beginning years (1931-1936) were women who graduated from elite colleges like Wellesley, Smith, Reed, or Radcliffe. Once they graduated from Bank Street, private progressive schools recruited most of them.

Most students at CST were different from the typical Normal School or other college students. The majority of the students at the CST had a bachelor's degree, whereas most standard teacher education students were undergraduates. From the available data about the cohort of 32 students in 1934-1935, at least nine majored in English; others majored in French, mathematics, history, and psychology. They were educated in prestigious colleges. For instance, students graduated from Wellesley, Smith, Vassar, the Sorbonne (Paris), Mount Holyoke, Bryn Mawr, Barnard, Bowdoin, Bennington, Sarah Lawrence, the University of Michigan, and Ohio State University. This array suggests a rather different social class background from the reported background of students in most Normal Schools.

There is some partial information about 23 students, out of 32, for the year 1934-1935 (Annual Report). In spite of having the names of the students, part of their personal information remained confidential and could not be matched with the information provided in the table below.

Figure 1: Students' Educational Background

Student #	Institution	Degree	Major
1	Elmira, NY	BS	Mathematics, Physics
2	Vassar	AB	Art
3	Iowa State College	2 Semesters	English
	State Univ. of Iowa	1 Summer	English
4	New Jersey College for Women	BS	Home Economics
5	Pennsylvania College for Women	BA	English
	Univ. of Michigan	MA	Literature
6	Trinity College	BA	
7	Wellesley	BA	Music
8	Wellesley	BA	English
	Ohio State Univ.	1 year	Literature
9	Wellesley	BA	Literature
10	Smith	BA	French
	Sorbonne, Paris	Degree Superior	
11	Univ. of Texas	BA	English, Coomp. Lit.
12	Bennington	2 years	Child Psych.
13	Sorbonne, Paris	1 year	French, History
14	Vassar	B.A.	Child Studies
15	Bryn Mawr	BA	French
16	Elmira	BS	Sociology, Nutrition
17	Sarah Lawrence	BA	Religion, Psych., German
18	Wellesley	BA	Mathematics
19	Barnard	BA	Fine Arts
20	Mount Holyoke	BA	English
21	Bowdoin	AB	Psychology
22	Smith	1 year	English
23	Mount Holyoke	BA	History

The age of the students also differed from the prospective teachers in traditional programs. Most students were in their mid-twenties, ranging from age nineteen to thirty-eight for the in 1934-1935 school year. For instance, for the year 1934-1935 six of the 32 students were married, the median age for all the students was 23 (which means that half of the students were younger and the other half were older than 23) while the average was almost 25 (Annual Report, 1934-1935). Further, in their selection, CST was careful to look for students with life experience in diverse fields and in diverse places and with interest in a variety of issues from social to artistic.

The number of students in the program during the 1930s was small, ranging from 22 for the 1931-1932 academic year to 35 in the late 1930s. The small size of the group allowed for a cohort and community effect. During the program, students had an intense common experience that created a bonding situation. As a student referring to her experience in 1932-1933 put it,

> We were such a small group that we were one, and we went through everything together. We just had one schedule of courses that we all took.... Well, that class of ours had a lot of people of different ages I would say. I think there were some older. Not many younger. How old was I? In the early twenties. But we all shared this excitement. Oh, we'd go out and have dinner together in some little restaurant. I would say we were a good group of people who liked each other. We were all most thrilled by this marvelous year we were having.
>
> Lewis, 3/26/75, p. 34.

CHAPTER THREE

Curricular Organization

Program Form and Content

The Cooperative School for Student Teachers had a perception of program organization in which there should not be a division between practical and conceptual work since the practical was perceived as a highly intellectual activity and the conceptual could not be elaborated without grounding theory from experiential situations. Thus, for one academic year, students were placed in school settings from Monday until Thursday as teacher's assistants. During this same year, from Thursday evening until Saturday afternoon they attended classes, for an estimated 12 to 15 weekly hours, that aimed at supporting their work in classrooms as well as enhancing their understanding of the larger context of schooling. There was variation of contact hours between students and faculty in the program throughout the year, which changed according to the number of classes offered at certain periods of the year, the number of weeks that these classes lasted, and the intensity of weekly hours for each class. The program lasted one academic year for each cohort of about 30 students. Few students enrolled in one or two classes on a part-time basis. There was a second-year option for an on-going seminar. The content of the curriculum was organized through courses at the Greenwich Village (New York) location of the BEE where also a nursery school lab and a research center functioned.

As mentioned above, the Cooperative School curriculum was organized to provide students with two major centers of learning: (a) classroom experience with children, and (b) a sequence of professional courses in education and child development. Thus, the practice-teaching happened from the beginning of the academic year and throughout the year, four days a week (Mondays to Thursdays). At the same time, students attended organized seminars, discussion courses, and field trips for two full days a week (from Thursday evening to Saturday afternoon. The intensity of this program demanded total commitment on part of the students with the understanding that the time constraints meant no chance to have a paid job elsewhere during this year-long program (from the end of September to the beginning of June).

The first activity that students had on Thursday evenings was dance and corporal expression. This dance activity was also a way of conveying a message about the interconnection of body, soul, and mind. Several courses at CST focused on the arts. Music, plastic arts, drawing, and even wood shop, were part of the core curriculum. Furthermore, this program prepared teachers in direct connection with alternative and experimental teaching, a children-centered curriculum and child development, curriculum development, field trips, artistic expression through dance, play, music, sculpture, and writing, extensive field experience in progressive schools, teachers' inquiry, personal introspection, and active civic and social participation. Courses focused on systematic research through qualitative methods and systematic inquiry into and evaluation of one's own practice. In addition, the curriculum offered an array of short courses on social theory and political issues taught by faculty from the New School for Social Research such as Max Lerner, editor of the magazine "The Nation." The description of the class on "Environment" will expand this short description. The following section presents the curriculum of teacher preparation at Bank Street, and describes the program structure, the courses, and the dimensions of knowledge necessary for beginning teachers.

The Focus and Organization of the Curriculum

The idea of teacher preparation at Bank Street focused on the development of the prospective teacher as a person and as a professional. The profound intellectual respect that the program showed toward its students shaped the curriculum content. Teachers should be independent and critical thinkers who foster a habit of inquiry and reflection to understand their practices. As "The Students of the Cooperative School 1934-35" (1935) wrote: "None of us is leaving Bank Street with a packet of ideas neatly sealed and ready to be pigeon-holed. We all have the feeling that given the Cooperative School as a Springboard, there is no limit to where one can leap" (p. 2). Teachers cannot be provided just with a set of techniques, but rather with the skills and habits to reinterpret their practices and validate and challenge their own constructions of meaning and knowledge. Bank Street program assumed that the best education a teacher can get should enable her/him to teach by fostering the habits of inquiry and reflection, and by the habit of lifelong learning and personal and professional development. Thus, the experiences in their program, its curriculum and pedagogy, the knowledge and meanings for teaching were structured to accomplish such outcomes.

The way in which the sequence of courses, practice-teaching, and other experiences were organized responded to the perceived needs of the student-teachers. It focused on their growth as persons and in their development as professionals. Figure 2 below will give an idea of how the curriculum used a developmentalist approach to the preparation of teachers. It is such in the sense that the timing of different courses during the school year is meant to be in accordance to the perceived needs and concerns of the student teachers and of the practice-teaching experience. Also, it provides a sense of different courses and the curricular areas covered. The dotted lines represent when the course started and its length. Class meetings were once a week and usually lasted about two hours (Catalog, 1933-1934). Course-work started on Thursday evenings and continued on Fridays and Saturday mornings. Practice-teaching occurred parallel and in connection to the course-work.

Figure 2: Schedule of Classes Through the Academic Year

October	November	December	January	February	March	April	May	June
Environment---(preparation)-Trip-(closure)------	
Observation and Record Taking----	
The Development of Personality---	
The Dance---	
Design Workshop-------------	
Topics in Child Development-------------	
Curriculum Planning for Older Children-----------	
Language----------------------	
Curriculum for Younger Children---------	
Map Making (6 sessions)
Techniques of Tool Subjects (6 sessions)
Dramatics and the Voice (15 sessions)
Shop----------------	
Music--------------------------	
Practice -Teaching---	

The program lasted one academic year, from October to June. Practice-teaching was a student teaching experience where the prospective teacher was in a classroom every week for the whole year from Monday to Thursday. Unfortunately, I have not enough data to provide evidence about the nature of the student-teacher experience in the school classroom, the type of relationships, the instructional assignments, or the role of the classroom teachers in connection to the Bank Street student. However, coursework supported the field experience and the class on "personality" played an important aspect of learning about oneself vis-à-vis interactions with students and other adults --colleagues, directors, and/or families and community, as well as the environment.

The coursework was planned to provide "sequences in curriculum organization corresponding to the student's maturing professional growth and classroom experience with children" (Outline, 1937, p. 17). The first concern in the curricular sequence was student-teachers' need to understand children and to understand themselves in relation to children. After the student-teachers gained understanding and felt comfortable in the company of children, and after they examined themselves in relation to children and gain an understanding of the context (the school, the community, the world), the focus shifted to the professional aspects of being a teacher. In this stage, courses concentrated more on technical problems, teaching methods, selection of materials, and curriculum planning. Actually, the course on Curriculum Planning was used as an integrating unit also for the organization of a year curriculum for the grade in which the student was teaching or going to teach. Further, this course was taught during the time that the "Environment" (social studies course) started to focus on the connections between content and children learning.

> The close relation which the Cooperative School curriculum undertakes to maintain between theory and practice, course-work and classroom experience, inevitably makes somewhat artificial any arbitrary division of the curriculum into discreet courses. In fact, in order to reduce such arbitrary dividing lines to a minimum, the course schedule itself is consciously organized so that courses which are closely related in content and purpose are scheduled at contiguous periods [and]...are planned and scheduled to constitute organically related elements within basic seminars of content rather than isolated individual units of instruction.
>
> Outline, 1937, p. 16

This connection also facilitated the actual implementation of the student-teachers' planning for the classrooms. This was an essential part of their curriculum since the actual value of the planning was to be tested by its consequences in a real setting, which is a pragmatist perspective. This meant also that the complexity of actual teaching had a strong impact on the ways in which the following activities were organized. This was a situational-contextual problem-issue approach in which the consequences of the act of teaching were scrutinized for further learning, judgment, and action.

Knowledge for Teaching

Bank Street emphasized that teachers must understand and enjoy children. Also, teachers should know the world in which children live and understand the social, political, and economic contexts which condition the environment in which children grow and develop. This assumes a need for the teachers' own social perspectives to be explored and the need for teachers to engage actively as a participant in social and civic responsibilities. This meant that teachers should be active in the shaping of a nurturing and just society for the healthy growth and needs of children as well as adults. This necessary disposition and knowledge for teaching comes from the perspective that there is a need for understanding the contemporary world because there was

> [E]vidence that the experiences which determine the educational development of the child are not confined to the school but relate equally to the whole amount of experiences outside the school--in the home and elsewhere--by which humans beings undertake to satisfy their basic needs for food, clothes, houses, health, economic security, satisfying social relations, recreation, and creative expression.
>
> Outline, 1937, pp. 3-4.

In addition, the prospective teacher must know the principles and philosophy, as well as the curriculum methods and materials of the schools which represented creative, progressive, experimental, and child-centered practices (particularly in early childhood and early elementary education). The most advanced, adventurous, and challenging practices constituted "the raw material out of which the student forges her own standards of professional competence and achievement" (Outline, 1937, p. 4). The four major areas of personal and professional interest that served as the centers of organization around which the different courses were grouped were (Outline, 1937; Teacher Education Curriculum, 1938):

1. Learning the self as a person who teaches: This referred to the personal dimension of the teacher in understanding the self as a person and as a professional and the quality of the teaching relation. What should teachers be like? What are the desirable personal dispositions of teachers? How can teachers' needs be nurtured to foster or enhance their intellectual, social, and emotional dispositions and effectiveness to support children's learning?

2. Learning the world: This referred to the study of social issues and the role of the school as a social institution. What is the world like? What are the social and economic forces that condition the every-day world in which children live in? How do the cultural, social, political, and economic contexts affect the life of the home and school as social institutions concerned with the life of children?

3. Learning about children: This meant the learning of child development and child psychology. What are children like? What does it mean to be a child? What are the basic characteristics of child development? What are the needs of the children for a healthy growth? What are the learning processes of children at different stages of development?

4. Learning about the school: What should schools be like? What is the curriculum content? What are the methods of teaching? How is the school organized? How is the curriculum organized in different grades and for different children? Upon which principles is the curriculum organized? What are philosophical and psychological perspectives that shape the curriculum, the methods of instruction, and the selection of materials to stimulate learning processes?

These centers of organization or dimensions are rather arbitrary since many courses covered most or all of these aspects. Furthermore, many experiences integrated and melted the boundaries of these dimensions.

Nevertheless, for explanatory reasons and for structuring the understanding of these very same dimensions, they are presented separately with some examples from the content in a few courses.

Learning the Self

The first dimension of the curriculum focused on the development of the person. Courses like Dramatics, Music, Dance, Shop, or Design Workshop, were spaces to enrich and develop emotions and sensitivities.

> In The Dance and in Dramatics we became aware of our bodies as vehicles of expression, of the subtleties in the curve of the little toe, and of the hypnotic possibilities of a voice from the diaphragm. Mr. Pearson (art) allowed us no preconceptions about design as we played a little grimly with line, color and mass. Those of us who had never written a note before emerged from Music with not only a whole song of our own composing but also words to go with it, and much better ears for D and D sharp.
> The Students of the Cooperative School 1934-1935, 1935, p. 2.

These courses for the student-teachers were also an opportunity to do some creative work and to make connections with children's learning. The process of engaging in creative art was important because it was assumed that it would help the student-teacher better understand what children experience when engaging in these activities and to value the importance of emotion, sensitivity, and creativity in the growth of the child. For instance, the course on Dramatics, taught by Charlotte Perry, made explicit that its content would cover "Materials and methods for use with different age levels and backgrounds and for different types of school and class groups. Use of symbols and underlying rhythms as teaching methods" (Catalog, 1933-1934).

The course that focused on personality and part of the course on environment had also as objectives the development of the self.

> It was pure education for the person who was there. We did have a course or two called tool subjects, which would be teaching reading, writing and arithmetic, but most of it was that we were being developed as people, which, of course, was tremendously exciting.
> Kerlin, 7/14/75, p. 3.

Learning to teach implied learning the self since personal and social qualifications of the teacher determine the nature of the relationships built in the classroom and in the school community. While the developmentalist perspective to curriculum shaped this view, it was also shaped by the contemporary psychoanalytic perspectives in education that advocated for self-exploration and introspection as means of individual growth (Biber, 7/14/75). Therefore, the curriculum was concerned not just with providing opportunities to nurture the sensibilities of the prospective teacher and but also with providing rich personal experiences.

> ...you hoped that you could help the students see how they as people were relating to this profession. What in their background really led them to it, what in their background supported it, where their greatest satisfactions were, where there were problems that could be worked out, and you should be able to help them.
>
> Biber, 8/13/75, p. 13.

This self-exploratory and autobiographical approach was incorporated in the personality class (taught by Elizabeth Healy).

> In the large group discussion with miss Healy most of us were able to say--probably for the first time in our lives --what we really were thinking; and we learned that we were neither so bad as we had feared nor so good as we had hoped; and, what may be more important, that the other person had fears and hopes not so very different from our own. Nor were these meetings limited to our interest in ourselves; every meeting included children; as a matter of fact, we are willing to swear that no other class had ever integrated their entire experience so beautifully.
>
> The Students of the Cooperative School 1934-1935, 1935, p. 1.

To use their words, they were concerned with the mental hygiene of the teacher and the teaching relation. Thus, the curriculum had to address these needs:

> As an aspect of its basic concern with the personality development of the teacher, the Cooperative School recognizes that mental health and maturity are not something which can be achieved by individual efforts of will. Skill on the professional job is essential to the feeling of well-being and matured assurance which frees the teacher to establish an easy, flexible and constructive educational relationship with children.
>
> Outline, 1937, pp. 2-3.

Therefore, learning the self was also about inquiring into oneself as one of the students remembers this aspect of learning about the self:

> Every week ended with a two hour session with her (Elizabeth Healy). We sat in a circle and she brought out the psychological aspects of our becoming teachers... The whole purpose was not to examine you, but just to open up possibilities to you, and when we came out, we were aware of ourselves.
>
> Killan, 2/20/76, p. 8.

Learning the World

A second dimension of the curriculum was the need for students to learn about the world. It built, connected, and inter-played with the personal development while learning about themselves through the arts and self-explorations. The connection between learning the self and learning the world was manifested by the expectation that Bank Street students would explore and start to define their own social perspectives and the expectation that the prospective teachers will engage in social, community, and political activities outside the school settings to farther the improvement of social conditions. This was another way to work and advocate in favor of children (in addition to classroom teaching) by influencing the larger social context in which children grow. As a faculty member summarized: "We were in education because we thought there was a way to make a better world" (Biber, 7/21/75, p. 7). Learning the world, thus, became necessary for the students to be able to change it, and teaching was a way of changing it.

But teaching in itself was not enough. As discussed in prior chapters, there was a strong concern with the social and economic contexts in which children grew and the influence of these contexts on the teaching job, the 1930s were particularly hard for the economy, and the country embraced the New Deal as a response to the impact of the Depression. The idea that teachers should be socially active responded to the socio-historical context. The faculty at Bank Street saw teaching as part of a larger movement for social change.

> I was also very much concerned in those days, as I think many of us were, with the directions in which America was going ...It was the early days of the CIO which had grown out of the American Federation of Labor... We had a good strong labor organization in

this country and we were going to help strengthen its fabric in democratic ways. I have to confess, I've since changed my mind a little bit. There was a lot of social ferment in those days and concern about the problems of the Depression and all that Franklin Roosevelt had brought to the attention of the people.

Smith, 8/25/75, pp. 32-33.

Moreover, in an internal memo written in 1935, Eleanor Bowman (a faculty member) shared with her colleagues some of her perspectives on the program and called for Bank Street faculty to be active. She wondered:

> Also how much of an influence we can be unless we ourselves feel strongly enough about a new society to be willing to take part in building it. Isn't this influence an important factor in the learning process? Will we develop social attitudes in students unless we ourselves have a philosophy strong enough to be doing something about the condition of the world? (11/12/35, p. 1)

Her commitments were not just about teaching but also about being actively involved in changing social arrangements. However, her concerns were also curricular and pedagogical. She wanted these perspectives to be part of the student-teacher experiences. She also wanted to model activism to the students at Bank Street. The potential involvement of the faculty was important, so that future teachers would learn from the examples of active engagement. In this view, what was taught and said should be the basis for one's actions.

The course on Environment did much to promote this kind of learning. The course, which will be discussed in the next chapter, focused on learning the community, its patterns, and the social, geographical, and economic characteristics. It was used for learning to teach social studies, for learning to do research, and for learning firsthand social issues. Toward the end of the year there was a field trip to the "coal areas" of Pennsylvania and West Virginia, and to Washington. On this trip students learned more about geology, animal life, social conditions, unionization, the role of the government, educational consequences at large, and teaching implications among other things.

However, besides the content covered in the course on Environment, there was an urgency to provide extra experiences outside the regular settings. This goal was partly met through special meetings and lectures. However, it was fundamentally met through actual work in community projects. This approach had an impact on the students. In another undated internal memo where (probably prepared through in 1936 or 1937) a group of four students whose names are difficult to read because they are handwritten (probably they were Bjorling, Pat Clark, Ch. Hall, and Patsy Bageley), wrote the following:

> We believe that a teacher's job is not only in the classroom. That while a teacher's primary responsibility is to help children grow and develop to the best of their potentialities, she has a responsibility also for the kind of world these children are growing up in. She cannot ignore the influences outside the classroom that are shaping children's lives. And so the students at Bank Street spend a portion of their time working with local community agencies on some of the pressing problems in our neighborhood. Different members of the staff are close to these problems through their membership and participation on various local committees and the students share in any of this work that seems appropriate to their interest and experience. This year we are continuing our effort for a low income housing project. We are working with Greenwich House on their health program. We are cooperating with a public school in their after school recreation activities and we are running a Saturday Play group for neighborhood children. (p. 1)

In 1937, the Environment course was divided into a new course and a new larger area of studies (Outline, 1937). The new course was School Use of Environment (geography, history, and social studies). The new larger area was called Contemporary Civilization and the Role of the School as a Social Institution. The four parts of this area of studies were: (a) Foundations of American Culture (1 hr. weekly, 15 weeks), (b) Social and Economic Problems in Relation to Education (1 hr. weekly, 15 weeks), (c) Field Work in Social Organizations and Community Agencies (3 hrs. weekly, 15 weeks and the trip described above), and (d) Current Educational Problems and Philosophies (2 hrs. weekly, 15 weeks). While I couldn't find in the different sources of data any specific description of the courses, it just makes sense to assume that some of the issues discussed above in this chapter were part of the content. Learning the world and acting upon and beyond teaching for changing the world was an integral part of learning to teach at Bank Street.

This dimension of learning to teach invites three commentaries. First, it challenges the perspective that student-centered curriculum missed the larger social context implications of schooling and the relevancy of these contexts for schooling and teaching. Bank Street seems to show that it is possible to further a developmentalist teacher education program with a child-centered orientation that also fosters a social reconstructionist perspective. Further, in her course on Child Development, Biber described the conception of theories as culturally and socially contextualized. Thus, she affirmed, "a lot of people feel that a lot of the theory is culture and time bound and is not as universal as it was made to be, so you began to look with a more social-cultural viewpoint" (Biber, 7/31/75, p. 19). Certainly, the social reconstructionist critiques penetrated the curriculum at Bank Street.

Second, it problematizes the critique of psychological developmentalist teacher education programs as narrow since such a program adds the dimension of social contextualization and social action to the developmental curriculum. Third, it reaffirms the metaphor of the teacher as a critical citizen (Ayers, 1991) in addition to the artistic, naturalistic, and inquiry oriented metaphors (Perrone, 1989) when thinking of a developmentalist and progressive teacher education program.

Learning About Children

Several courses and field-experiences aimed at helping the prospective teacher to gain a systematic understanding about children and about the connections between child development and teaching and learning. After all, Bank Street as an institution that developed out of the Bureau for Educational Experiments, which had as a main purpose the study of children. Since the belief was that school experiences were aimed at helping children learn and to nourish their healthy development, the teachers understanding of children as a different category of learners was a fundamental idea: "My feeling about teachers was: the more they understood about the sources of children's behavior, the better" (Biber, 7/31/75, p. 19).

Furthermore, it was necessary also to understand that children growth was developmental and that there were certain stages of growth that were different from each other. The course on Child Development explicitly addressed this concern:

> That effort in that course, really, in every way that I could, for myself and for the student, to integrate psychological theory of child development and human function with specific material about children in school at different stages of development. Of

course I was a stage development theorist from the beginning so the people who worked developmentally, like the ones I've said, like Werner and Piaget and so forth, who believed the basic premise that human development, child development doesn't proceed, you know, like the ruler, one inch, two inches, three inches, but there are certain blocks of development and from one block of development to the other there are very basic qualitative changes that isn't just that you could think more clearly when you were eight than when you were four. You think altogether differently at eight than when you are four -not a little bit more of the same. There are qualitative changes in all the functions from stage to stage. That's really what the basic stage developmentalists believe. Where I got that from is a combination of what I saw around me in the children, and what I read--theories that appealed to me.

Biber, 8/13/75, pp. 3-4.

Yet, the intention was not to be dogmatic about it, but to understand it and make connections with the implications for curriculum development and for teaching. The way in which, for instance, the course on Child Development or the course on Observation and Record Taking were conceptualized and taught demonstrates a strong concern for connecting the content with the practice of teaching. The importance of learning observational skills for teaching was not just for the purpose of developing researcher skills, it was primary "Because the basic idea was to see what the child is like before you figure out what his education should be" (Biber, 3/27/75, p. 25). The course on observation was originally taught by Harriet Johnson. After her death, Jessie Stanton, who also taught one of the Curriculum Planning sections, taught it. This course, as well as Child Development, followed the observation classes in order to have students with already developed skills that served them in these two areas of study. For instance, a student recalls that,

I did take the course in Observation of Children's Behavior (Harriet Johnson was the instructor)...She insisted that you look at the child, or the group, or whatever it was whose behavior you were observing, describing directly as possible, leaving out your interpretations, but just getting down what happens like a word moving picture. It was an awfully good exercise. She had us observing children in the group situation, and then a single child for the whole day. Then she had us listen to their language... So that you would be able, by describing children's behavior, to get closer to understanding what they were communicating, what they

> were telling us about themselves, what they were interested in, what confused them, about what they enjoyed, or what troubled them, before we began either condemning or praising or interpreting. Get the child's own message as directly as possible. People tended to -they didn't listen to children with all of their senses. This was a new idea to me.
>
> Beyer, 9/29/78, p. 11.

While in the observation course students were developing skills, in the other courses they started to learn to interpret. Particularly, the Child Development class provided the theoretical perspectives and frameworks to think about what it was that the observational data provided. Moreover, the information gathered by the students became part of the study and analysis so that student-teachers could build connections with real situations. We can see here another benefit of the intense practice-teaching component. Students contextualized their observations in terms of the situation and in terms of the theoretical frameworks. Moreover, these contextualized observations also enhanced the learning of other students in the class and that of the faculty teaching the course. A faculty member recalls that she,

> ...would ask the student to take some or one of those four lines of development, like language development or like social development, or like thinking or creative expression (the fourth one was probably creative expression). Take such a topic. Read everything about it you could, in the literature, but go in and observe that topic in the age level that you are in. So put your observations of a specific group of children on a given topic in an age level, against the background of the whole literature. That was not an easy thing to do...I would take the students' papers... Then when I went back to teach and I wanted to really feel I wasn't just teaching out of books, I would go back to that source material, and then it would enrich my own understanding from the students' work, so the students' work became a very important source for me for developing my own knowledge. I think that was one reason why when I taught, it remained alive. It was an interaction between what I was learning from the students, not only from what they had to say in class, which was also important, but by studying their work... You have different illustrations all the time.
>
> Biber, 8/13/75, pp. 2-3.

Furthermore, there was an intention to develop these habits of inquiry and interpretation in order to provide the prospective teacher with tools for decision making in classroom situations. As mentioned above, the cases provided material for analysis, discussion, and learning. The intention was also to look at things from multiple perspectives, to speculate with different ideas and reasons, to evaluate possibilities, to use the theoretical perspectives to construct meanings, and to think about the consequences of different actions. In a sense, this approach of practical reasoning which involves an inquiry oriented disposition on part of the teacher is necessary to deal with the uncertainties of teaching. For instance, Barbara Biber reflected on a situation she recalls in which a case of a child's aggression was discussed:

> The question is, is it important for the teacher, when the child becomes very aggressive, to entertain certain questions in her mind, what is behind this aggression. Because aggression, if you go back to thinking of multiple theories, you have multiple explanations. Maybe it's this, maybe it's that. Maybe it's the other. Not because you're a dope and don't know what to think, but because you're highly informed and you realize that aggression is a behavioral act which even for any one child can have any of a number of causations, and if you become so bound to one theory that every time you see a child be indifferent about the doll that he's playing with and let it lie on the floor, and if you're so bound to orthodox Freudian theory that all you can see there is sibling rivalry, then I consider you a very limited figure, from my point of view. If a child just leaves a doll lying on the floor, then if your background is full, you should be able to think of about four different possible reasons, and not be sure which is the reason at that moment. That is not a very easy way to be a teacher.... Being able to think of multiple causes. Taking as a primary principle of psychology behavior has multiple causes, in general and in particular, and having a rich enough background so you can think. Now, as a teacher, at any given moment, you have to make some decision. But when you make that decision, it should not be an absolute one. You make a decision: This is probably what is the matter. The sensible thing is to do this. Then watch and see the effect of what you do, and if it doesn't have an effect, go back and think. I was on the wrong track. If you are orthodox, with one theory, you can't do that.
>
> Biber, 7/31/75, p. 20.

Therefore, as noted before, learning about children was also important for learning about the ways in which the classroom environment could be organized. The better teachers understand children, the better teachers understand themselves, the better they understand the local and the world contexts of the students and the community, the better are the chances that the teaching will be educational.

Learning About the School

The fourth dimension of the teacher education curriculum was learning and understanding about school life. It focused on planning the school/classroom environment and on the practice of teaching. Courses like Environment or Map Making or Language provided new organizations and structures to think about subject matter. Since in some minor measure this classes made also explicit the processes of content organization and their pedagogies, they also served as arenas for learning to teach. Furthermore, it was assumed that student-teachers would learn from the modeling provided in such courses, which many times were only implicit models of teaching. Other experiences like the Techniques of Tool Subjects or the Curriculum classes and the practice-teaching experience provided much content in this dimension.

For instance, the Curriculum for Younger Children studied "the organization of the classroom program for children from two through seven" (Catalog, 1933-1934, no page number). This class covered the need to play and the routines of classroom life, uses of blocks, story-telling, organization of trips, among other themes in order to give the student-teacher concrete skills for the classroom. In the Curriculum Planning for Older Children (eight through twelve), there was far more focus on using social studies as a base for the curriculum. In this class students had to design concrete curriculum. The developed plans served partly for implementation and practice during their practice-teaching experiences. However, since a big part of the planning was done toward the end of the program, the designed curriculum aimed at the possible school and age group the prospective teacher would probably teach the next year.

While in the 1933-1934 school year there were only six class meetings to help students with the 'tool subjects" (arithmetic, spelling, reading, writing) soon Bank Street realized that there was a piece of knowledge missing. In part, the assumption was that students could acquire this knowledge and skills during their practice-teaching experience from the daily work with the classroom teachers and/or with the aid of the school director. In most cases it didn't happen. Besides, Bank Street also realized the need for a better approach to the conceptualization of the subjects themselves. Faculties from some neighboring institutions were invited to teach some of these classes. For instance, according to a letter sent by R. Smith dated April 3rd, 1937, to Madeleine P. Grant, who was a professor at Sarah Lawrence College, she taught science/human biology in the Cooperative. At least, in terms of time, in the 1937 curriculum outline the so called "tool subjects" (reading, writing, arithmetic, spelling) were given 15 meetings of two hours (weekly) in contrast to six meetings in the past and in addition to the creative writing class.

Furthermore, the new Outline (1937) separated "Environment" into the social studies area (including geography and history) for teaching purposes (as before, 15 meetings of 2 hrs.) and into Contemporary Civilization (described above in the "learning the world" section).

CHAPTER FOUR

"Teaching Like That"

Understanding the complexity of teaching and learning to teach required an approach that was rather problem/issue based, contextualized, tailored, and evaluated by its effects. This process led to a practical reasoning that captured the expected skill level of teachers at Bank Street from teachers. For example, Barbara Biber, a faculty member who taught "Child Development" in the teacher education program, asserted that:

> You should understand everything you can about child development: Conscious, unconscious, developmental, Piaget, everything, but there had to be some clarity about how the teacher should act on this knowledge. That is a very difficult point, and I can't say that I can define exactly what it is. If you give me a case instance, I'll always know whether I think it's right or wrong. It's very hard to make a general theory about it. (Biber, 3/27/75)

Thus, practical reasoning aimed at "give me a case instance," and with the knowledge form theory and practice the teacher would evaluate alternatives, act, and again evaluate consequences. Consistent with Dewey's arguments about reflectivity (1933), this approach was generated through a systematic scientific inquiry grounded in the study of experience (Dewey, 1938). The following section provides two examples of teaching at Bank Street.

The two examples chosen are the teaching of "Environment" and the teaching of "Language," both taught by Lucy Sprague Mitchell. The two courses provide two very different areas of content from which some commonalties about teaching could be inferred. These classes give a sense of the nature of the interactions and of the ways in which knowledge was conveyed and constructed. Besides, the two classes provide an interesting context in which an "educative experience," in Dewey's terms, is attempted in the preparation of teachers. To help explain the processes of these courses, four intertwined dimensions of learning to teach at Bank Street are used: (1) learning the world, (2) learning about children, (3) learning the "school" (curriculum, routines, subject matter, environments), and (4) learning the self as a teacher (Curriculum Plans, 1934-1935).

Teaching the Class on 'Environment'

The class on "Environment" focused on one of Lucy Sprague Mitchell passions: Human Geography. This course enabled students to build several complex connections. First, it aimed at furthering students' understanding of Human geography, the ways in which knowledge is constituted and validated, and how it connects to other areas of geography and of social studies. Second, it aimed at developing the habit of systematic inquiry into the obvious, the everyday life, of communities, neighborhoods, and society at large. Third, it aimed at providing students with the concrete tools to help children learn the subject. It required, in Bank Street perspective, a profound understanding of children and how children learn, as well as a deep understanding of school life, curriculum, and the organization of the environment for learning. Fourth, it also aimed at developing awareness about learning and understanding on part of the student-teacher. The learner had to experience learning and then make explicit the processes in order to inquire about it (Outline, 1937).

In this course on Environment, students started studying the school community (neighborhood), as well as the local community where they were placed for practice-teaching. During the first part of the course, each student investigated, observed, conducted interviews, and also used other sources of information as, for instance, statistics, journal articles, and magazines. The projects ranged in topics such as food, housing, everyday routines of people, businesses, institutions, and life conditions. These experiences allowed them to start the process of making conceptual connections about social and material relationships in the community and the influences on the school setting in order to analyze cultural patterns of the community where the school was located. By the end of this line of fieldwork, students organized in study groups and concentrated in a contemporary social issue relevant for the community. Study groups analyzed the historical, geographical, cultural-ethnic, and economic backgrounds. Upon this study (learning the world), the focus shifted to how to use this knowledge in teaching children (learning about children and learning the "school"): "On the trips around New York, apparently we were also thinking about children's trips; what they would see" (Tarnay, 7/8/75, p. 10).

Students at Bank Street were expected to build understanding of these issues by connecting them with the possible influences on the families of the children, on the children, and on themselves as teachers (all the dimensions of learning to teach). A student recalls:

> I had not thought of teaching in these terms. I hadn't really thought of it so much as part of developing your own concepts of what goes on in the community, and really going in and finding out what really was going on, how -this affected your own teaching. Well, it affected the kids and the parents if you were teaching in the same area.
>
> Schonborg, 6/11/76, p. 7.

After the 1933-1934 academic year, the course expanded in content, and more faculty were involved in its teaching. Besides Lucy Sprague Mitchell, Eleanor Hogan took some responsibilities for the design of the course. Also, Max Lerner was regularly involved in the teaching of this class, who at the same time was a faculty member at The New School for Social Research and the director of the political magazine 'The Nation," (Annual Report, 1934-1935). It incorporated more formally what could be called nowadays social studies and social foundations. This way the subject of human geography was expanded to accommodate several of the relationships within and among these fields of study. One of the implications of this expansion was the building of a stronger connection with the course on Curriculum, which focused in the development of school curriculum and the design of learning environments. An added focus, then, was that student-teachers developed social studies curriculum for classroom teaching: "We all wrote a social a studies curriculum, which I used the next year when I taught. I wrote one... I did it on the continent of Africa, with ancient Egypt as a kind of center..." (Schonborg, 6/11/76, p. 13). The idea of combining assignments provided an opportunity to integrate the content learned in meaningful ways. This integration, however, had to be open enough to respond to the student-teacher needs:

> It should be mentioned that courses, although planned in outline in advance, are intentionally left flexible in many details so that they

may readily be adapted to student needs as motivation indicates a heightened potential around particular content. Otherwise teaching runs the risk of following pre-conceived formal outlines of subject matter content at the expense of stultified learning. On the assumption that the felt needs of the learner, including purposeful exposure to new problem-raising experiences, should be the primary criteria in determining content and method, any other procedure would appear to be not only poor pedagogy but unfortunate example.

Outline, 1937, p. 18.

Moreover, the Environment course was also expanded with a new element: a long field trip to rural, industrial, and mining areas was added during the spring. As a student recalls:

Well, we had people like Max Lerner talking to us about social problems, we got all involved in the whole issue of unions and unionization and social justice and we went around with social workers to see what it was like to live in tenements. We explored Grand Central Station to see how it was built and how it worked. We did all kinds of trips and all kinds of experiences in the environment of New York. I remember walking down to the river from Bank Street and looking at the West Side Highway, which was then new. Then we went on the long trip, which was fantastic.

Kerlin, 7/14/75, p. 3.

The trip became a central event and a powerful experience in the Bank Street curriculum. It required a careful preparation in which students developed their own questions. The trip provided a unique opportunity to experience firsthand the complexity of some social issues outside the New York area. Furthermore, the trip was also used for learning firsthand geological themes, topography, geography, flora, and fauna of the region visited, and to build connections between these fields of study and the social and economic contexts. Another student remembers that:

When we went down to the coal country, there was a lot of background that was spent. We had lots of background on that place. Lucy, geographically, Eleanor the economics of that whole coal area; there was a lot of background before we even got there... We met a lot of miners. We all became members of the bootleg miners union. They were striking. They had flooded and closed some mines. The men were all out of work.

Schonborg, 6/11/76, p. 13.

After visiting the mining and rural areas, during the Roosevelt presidency, the trip took them also to the nations' capital with the purpose of better understanding social policy and its implications for education. Because of the personal relationship between Lucy Sprague Mitchell and Eleanor Roosevelt, the president's wife, it was possible to have Ms. Roosevelt as a guide (Cohen, 7/7/75). A. Killian, a student in the program, adds the following about the trip:

> Then we went from there to Washington, DC, and again Eleanor Roosevelt was with us and introduced us to, probably -the Department of the Interior or the Department of Labor or both, so that we could question the officials as to what was done for and with the miners' condition, and things like that. So you see, we'd been on this trip for four or five nights, and then rolled back into New York.
>
> Killan, 2/20/76, p. 11.

Back in New York, the focus was on building connections. First, the objective was to reinforce the concept of 'relational thinking," or connecting ideas, which meant that the environment was more than science or social studies: "It was more a matter of expressing what they experienced in order to understand it in the intellectual sense" (Labowitz, 8/8/75, p. 12). Second, the purpose was to further the connections with children's learning. After the student-teachers learned the content, understood relationships, and had a powerful personal experience that helped them construct personal meanings, they had to plan the environment to provide their own students in their particular classrooms with concrete experiences that will further learning. Again, Killan (2/20/76) recollects:

> But that was only the beginning of our trip! After that we had to put it into drama form, play form, art form, letters to the editors form, letter to our constituents. Everything. I wrote a little play about it, which was not good as a play, but it represented my feeling. We had really seriously experienced what children experience when they are trying to learn something new. That was the highlight. (p. 11)

This is one of the conceptual aspects of the role of experience at Bank Street: Student-teachers experienced what children might have experienced. Student-teachers also moved beyond the experience itself. Becoming aware, evaluating, analyzing, and thinking how to build the connection for teaching is what made this concept powerful. This process of inquiry into the experience incorporated an analysis and an evaluation of consequences. Experience per se, as Dewey (1938/1963) argued, is not necessarily educative. Thus, going beyond the experience, revising and analyzing it, was an important aspect of learning to teach.

An expected outcome of the experience was to scrutinize and to frame ideas and knowledge gained in order to connect them with children's learning by also understanding the relationships and processes by which the content was conveyed. A student at the time recalled:

> When we came back from our long trip, we had to prepare for our final. Our final was a question which we had to answer, and the question was "Can human nature be changed?" The class was broken up into a number of committees, which I think you could choose to be in. The committees had to look at different aspects of this; for example, some were looking at the biological and some were looking at it from the point of view of psychology, some politically, and some sociologically. There were four or five different committees whose work was to tackle this question from its particular vantage point. Then we spent at least two days in which each committee reported on what it had uncovered about this question, "Could human nature be changed?" And at the end of the whole thing there was a resounding "yes!" -complete agreement. As though a Bank Street group would come up with any other answer than that!
>
> Cohen, 7/7/75, pp. 30-32

The above quote fully captures the impact of the trip and its following experiences in terms of content, ideas, connections, and teaching. The Environment course provided students with chances to experience and inquire about the different dimensions of learning to teach at Bank Street–learning the self, learning about the world, learning about children, and learning about "schools."

Teaching the Class on "Language"

The teaching of language was based upon the idea that the teachers should be writers, or at least experiment with writing in systematic and critical ways. Lucy Sprague Mitchell created a community of writers where their own writing was exposed and criticized. An example of this, from a transcript called "Mrs. Mitchell's class in language," dated October 17, 1931, follows (pp. 3-4).

The class was discussing some examples of writing from some students in it. The conversation was led by Lucy Sprague Mitchell:

> Mrs. Mitchell [Reading from Catherine Shakespeare's paper] : . . . a morning sail-boat nearly turns over. Did you get any image?
>
> Group: Yes...Taste, smell, sound, tactual, etc.
>
> Mrs. Mitchell: When you wrote that, Miss Shakespeare, did you write naturally?
>
> Miss Shakespeare: I had to think back and feel them before I could write them.
>
> Mrs. Mitchell: Sometimes it is good to pantomime a situation. Three years old couldn't recall this, because it was beyond them... They couldn't think back without leaning. They practically live it back... When you say 'eyes are closed,' in a small child you almost see a motion of the eyes. Let's try it. Let go and see what sensation you have. (Examples: A fierce lion. A baby kitten. A strong draught horse.) To the extent that Miss Shakespeare was dominated in these images, she probably had literal muscular recalls... [Reads Mrs. MacCormack's exercise.] . . . Driving on Flourtown road. Has collision at intersection . . ..
>
> Mrs. Mitchell: Is this imagery?
>
> Group: No.
>
> Mrs. Mitchell: It is description, based on her imagery. I will read some more of these. Challenge each word. [Reads another exercise.]: Canary escapes from its cage. Is recovered.
>
> Miss Delcone: Some parts certainly are not direct, 'A sob burst from our lips.'
>
> Mrs. Mitchell: Suddenly she becomes the universal author. She becomes the impersonal and hears this sob. She becomes impassive.
>
> Miss Churchill: I think such words as 'gay.'
>
> Miss Bohn: Sometimes the English language doesn't provide words for a thing like that.
>
> Mrs. Mitchell: It is almost an introspective word. What could she have said to make the gayness purely the gayness of a canary?

The above excerpt from a transcript exemplifies several aspects of progressive teaching as defined earlier in this paper. First, there was a profound engagement with the subject matter. Second, there was a genuine interest in understanding the students' insights. (This was a must in order to help them gain knowledge) Third, the use of students' writing and ideas during instruction validated each student's work in a community of learners. Fourth, at the same time, the piece of work done by the student was challenged and it was used by everyone to learn from it. Fifth, it showed the level of respect and trust in this class since students were willing to share their work in public in spite of knowing that it would be challenged. Sixth, by doing these things, students were encouraged to rethink their writing and to improve it. Seventh, the student's ideas were developed by the class in order to think about how children might experience and build meanings. Eighth, besides sharing information about how children may experience or react, students exercised and simulated these feelings. They were encouraged to experience what children feel. Last, students participated and shared opinions in a dialogical mode. Yet the teacher focused them, questioned them, and moved them toward understanding.

This procedure also assumed the importance of modeling ideal teaching to prospective teachers (learning "school'). Making the process of teaching and learning part of the subject matter exposed prospective teachers not just to a different approach to experience learning, but also enabled their development as practitioners of this approach to teaching. The class was also an important vehicle to learn about children: If teachers had to write stories for children, it meant that they had to be serious students of how children think, of how children play, of how children feel, and of what it is like to be a child in these situations (learning about children).

The teaching of language and writing was a vehicle not only to learn more about childhood and language development, but also about the self. Teaching language and writing also possessed an aesthetic dimension. Part of the artistic creativity as a teacher also involved the ability to write (learning about the self).

Lucy Sprague Mitchell's teaching of writing was meaningful because as a teacher of teachers she pushed her students to improve their own writing (learning "school' and self). She was truly interested in her students and looked closely at their work. She made them think about their own writing and she offered multiple questions and perspectives in consistent ways with her understandings of what constituted good writing for children. As shown in the following example, in which she responded to a student poem, to be a student of her was a feast (Russel, 2/17/76, p. 2):

On Macy's Parade:
"Sleet stinging my face.
Wind, chilling me to the bone.
Feet, blocks of ice.
Eyes, dazzled by bright costumes.
Gargantuan figures.
Fantastic sights.
Boom-booming of drums.
Sleet. Wind. Walking on frozen feet.
Home. A warm fire. Peace"

And she (Mitchell) wrote the following comment:

You could push farther. 'Wind,' for instance. How did you know there was wind? Give your evidence. 'Peace.' Again, what evidence? 'Walking on frozen feet'-you leave the concrete images to reader. 'Fantastic,' in what way? 'Chilling me to the bone' has lost image quality by overuse. Good as far as goes, but go farther.

Russel, 2/17/76, p. 2.

For instance, Russel (2/17/76) recalls comments that she kept in writing from Lucy Sprague Mitchell about another exercise:

This is good material on a 5-yr.-old level, but it isn't organized or written in keeping with 5-yr.-old language and interest. The sentences are long and monotonous. Much unnecessary… something… thrown in. The episodes are not well set forth in direct language. Almost no pattern. If you don't know what I mean by the above remarks, let's have a conference.

Russel, 2/17/76, p. 2.

These responses were good examples of teaching from which students could learn. These examples also illustrate the centrality that the senses played in her views of writing. The poem is used to convey knowledge and feelings keeping an audience in mind. In addition, the ways in which she gave detailed feedback to her students could serve as a model to teachers of how to give feedback. Furthermore, Mitchell's pedagogy exemplified respect and caring for the learner (learning "school" in the sense of learning to relate to students). She didn't give up on the student, she wanted to push the student to improve, she had high expectations, she wanted the student to understand, and she was willing to take the time to help the student. The feedback was specific, concrete, and contextual to the work of the student.

She built on what the student did and what potentially he or she could have done but hasn't done yet. While directive in reference to possibilities, her feedback allowed room for the writers to express themselves without limits. The use of questions stimulates thinking, feeling, and provides guidance and focus to improve. These models provided insights and the necessary images from which to draw resources and ideas of good teaching and good writing.

Such emphasis on learning writing also connects to the perception of the teacher as one who constructs curriculum as well as develops it (learning school). In this perspective the future teachers cannot rely on prepackaged curriculums and materials. Reading stories with children was an important part of the curriculum in the experimental and progressive schools where these prospective teachers were going to teach (Sprague Mitchell, 1950; Winsor, 1973).

Because most of the stories written by Bank Street people were set in the here and now, they related to the world of the child in a specific context (learning the world). Thus, it is different to write a story for children with certain realities in the Appalachian mountains area and to write for children in a very different place like Greenwich Village (learning the world). The perspective was that a teacher should have the ability, skill, to write stories that would be relevant to the here and now of the children in the specific context in which the teacher and the children were situated. Consequently, for the teacher to be a writer was a required skill. It was a way of developing a meaningful and connected curriculum.

Learning "Language" also facilitated the learning of the self, in terms of personal development for the prospective teacher, and the world through aesthetic dimensions. Moreover, they enhanced the learning dimensions about children and about the world, gaining understandings about children's life contexts by writing poems and stories for them as audience. Ultimately, it also modeled approaches to the teaching of writing.

More Examples of Teaching

Examining the two courses "Environment" and "Language" gives a window into Lucy Sprague Mitchell's pedagogy and the pedagogy prospective teachers were being trained in. However, there is not much evidence about other instructors. There is some limited evidence about teaching in other courses based upon class syllabi. For instance, in the course on Human

Biology for Teachers, taught by Madeleine P. Grant, the syllabus highlights active science learning through experiences such as laboratory work, observation, handling of materials, dissections, and microscope work. Results were to be interpreted critically by the students. The emphasis in this course was on the use of the scientific method in practical and conceptual ways and to "Discover how much of this [the scientific] method is used by the child at different age levels" (Syllabi, 1936-1937). The length of the course consisted of 15 meetings of two hours each. Every class meeting had class presentation time or discussion, which preceded or followed laboratory work during the same meeting. The learning outcomes occurred in the class meetings, in the process of working in the lab and in discussing the scientific method. By the end of the course there was a practical quiz, but there is no evidence that this was the way to assess student outcomes. There is no record of grading and or of a reading list or assignments outside the class.

The syllabus on "Curriculum Planning for Young Children," is a hand-written document, has no name of instructor, and has no date. Since it was in the same box, in the archives, where the letter with the syllabus for the science class (1937) was located, probably this was the year written and, then, the instructor could have been Jessie Stanton. This valuable syllabus states that there will be teacher-directed discussions, and it also says that there will be "lectures illustrated with records from children's play, followed by discussions." In this course, there were assignments that were connected with the student-teacher practice teaching in the school setting. For instance, students in this course had to observe children and keep records of observation, create lists of play materials available, classify them, and document how and when children use them, observe and document teachers' behaviors and several teaching techniques. Besides documenting, there was an emphasis on conceptual work through analysis of field trips, description and analysis of different children in different curricular experiences, in terms of the needs of children at different ages, observe and report how the curriculum extends children's experiences, and analyze how teaching was used to help children to use language creatively and relate reading and play. Students also had to plan field trips and prepare an annotated bibliography of suitable books for different children at different age levels. The 15 classes in this course were arranged by blocks of age level (two-years-old, six-years-old, etc.) and by curriculum content, teaching techniques, activities, and children's books and materials. Attached to this syllabus is an extensive list of books and articles, but there is no evidence that any readings were assigned to the students in this course. The list of books ranges from books on child development to books that focused on specific curricular issues like art, music, science, or reading. Among the books, there were three authored by Harriet Johnson, the first director of the Bank Street Nursery, and "Before Books," co-authored by the same Jessie Stanton and by Caroline Pratt, the director of another progressive and experimental school, City and Country. However, there is no evidence of final papers or written assignments, or of systematic evaluation or grading. The only evidence available from the syllabus is that ongoing assignments were used as a learning tool and as ways of engaging in discussions and reflections.

These two syllabi provided some more insight into the teaching that took place at Bank Street. An important pattern showed in a heavy emphasis on process. The main learning happened during class discussion. While in the science course the main source of material for discussion was the laboratory work using the scientific method, in the curriculum class the main tool was classroom experiences in school settings. In both classes described through the syllabi, students engaged in gathering data and in making something out of it. Then, ideas and interpretations were debated and connections were made. From the evidence in these documents, it seems to be that since students had not read any bibliography, the instructor's authority figure in terms of ideas and conclusions debated was central for confirmation and validation.

A puzzling element is that of reading assignments. In the available documents from these syllabi there is no guide about what or when to read. In the science class there is no reading list at all. In the curriculum class, the bibliography is attached at the end, but there is no evidence that students read the books they were assigned or that they were discussed at all. An explanation could be that the list was used as a suggestion to the students.

Another syllabus to consider is that of Lucy Sprague Mitchell for the class on language and writing described above, in which there is no evidence of grading. However, she gave excellent feedback to the students' thirteen written assignments, which were designed to help students progress in their understanding of writing and they were also read in class. Some assignments focused on the use of the five senses for writing. The objective was to develop the artistic dimension of language and to move beyond language as logical communication. Another assignment asked students to write about rhythms such as "children running, a canoe ride, going to sleep," or using sounds, organizing plots, writing short stories and stories that use historical, geographical, and cultural information.

Toward the end of these 15 sessions, students had the chance to choose to write new stories for children or to improve writing that was started during the course. In terms of reading assignments, students read their writings and analyzed them in class. Also, the syllabus remarks that some classic works, e.g., by Homer and Shakespeare, would be read at the beginning of the course. There is a short, incomplete, bibliographical list that includes a book on children's language and works by Piaget. These readings make sense because of the subject matter of study. Most students had background in what was thought to be a good liberal education and many majored in English and literature, which explains why there was not much reading of literary works in this course. This syllabus is consistent with the other two in terms of final evaluation and reading assignments. However, this does not mean that they were not rigorous, demanding, and intellectually stimulating and exciting as, for instance, in the case of the final project after the long trip in the Environment class.

CHAPTER FIVE

The Idea of "Teaching Like That"

The idea of teaching at Bank Street was conceptualized from the following perspective: "the practical responsibility of creating a constructive educational relationship with children in which optimum learning may take place" (Outline, 1937, p. 7). Teaching refers to the activity of the teacher who fosters practices and interactions, which in turn engage and relate the learner to the content in order to promote growth and understanding.

> ...teaching is an interpersonal relations function. It isn't just a matter of transmitting knowledge and being very good about how to transmit knowledge. It is a way of one person, whether you're teaching children or whether you are teaching adults, somehow, in the way knowledge is communicated, the technique is transmitted, something happens between the people as people.
>
> Biber, 8/13/75, p. 5.

Recalling Lucy Sprague Mitchell teaching a geography lesson in a sixth grade that was labeled as a "difficult class," a student recalled: "Oh, the remark this child made ...When Lucy left the room was, 'That woman is a genius.' When the asked why, the child replied, 'Because she makes you know more than you think you could.' Which is what she did with all of us' (Kerlin, 7/15/97, p. 7). Teaching also refers to the practices that shape the building of the self as a knowledgeable individual. It is centered on the space created for learning in the particular situation in which there is a conversation, a dialogue between and among students and teachers about something. Thus, another aspect is the quality of the interpersonal and intersubjective dimensions of learning in relation to a subject of study. For instance, in learning writing, a student may ask: Who am I as a writer? Do I know how to write? Do I enjoy writing? Can I write? Why do I write? Why should I write? For what purposes? Who benefits from my writing? While learning how to write and the specifics of style, grammar, conventions, etc., the learner also develops a disposition and builds a self in relation to some way of knowing.

If teaching is perceived as an adventure, it also means that there is a degree of uncertainty. For teaching to explore and construct in relatively uncertain situations implies risk taking. Cohen (1988, p. 3) referring to Dewey's impact on ideas about teaching, wrote:

> This vision implied an extraordinary new conception of teaching... Teachers would then be able to devise ways for children to adventure their way to real knowledge... Teachers would have to become a species of mental mountaineer, finding paths between innocent curiosity and the great store of human knowledge, and leading children in the great adventures from one to the other.

This was an important element of the teaching at Bank Street because

> ...the teacher whose own intellectual processes were stimulated by new insights and discoveries would then make the analog and create for her children the same sense of excitement and discovery that she found for herself. That is if the teacher acquired a sense of the inter-relationship of the world in which they lived as grown-ups, then they could interpret to children the world in which they lived, and make it a vital, breathing, exciting setting in which history takes place.
>
> Black & Blos, 1961, p. 8.

Teaching was treated as a discipline, which means that scrutiny created critical opportunities for students of teaching to experience, conceptualize, analyze, and evaluate consequences. Two examples of teaching at Bank Street will be provided. The two examples chosen are the teaching of "Environment" and the teaching of "Language," both taught by Lucy Sprague Mitchell. There are several reasons why to use these two courses as examples. First, the two courses provide two very different areas of content from where some commonalties about teaching could be inferred. Second, Lucy Sprague Mitchell was the central figure of the program in its conceptualization and leadership. Third, the data available for these classes is ample and give a sense of the nature of the interactions and of the ways in which knowledge was conveyed.

The two courses were different in content and scope. They were also different in the way that they were taught. These courses illustrate different facets of structuring experiences and environments for learning. Yet, they share some common principles in the building of teaching relations. In the two courses there was emphasis on understanding how knowledge is constructed and validated. These two classes demonstrate the idea that the focus is the student as a knower and as constructor of knowledge.

Moreover, the two courses are concerned with making a strong connection between: (a) the ways in which the student-teachers were learning and the ways in which children learn; and (b) the content that was learned and the ways to construct a meaningful classroom environment for children to understand this content. The basic assumption about the nature of structured experiences discussed in the prior chapter is evident here again: Student-teachers have to experience learning and become aware of the ways in which they learned. Then, through careful analysis, they explored the nature of their own understanding to connect it with the ways in which children may make sense of their own experiences --of how children construct meaning and learn.

For most of the students at Bank Street this way of learning was a new experience. Passion, engagement, inquiry, the building of relationships and connections penetrated their conversations and experiences about teaching. Referring to Lucy Sprague Mitchell's teaching, a student recalled:

> I was so intrigued by her method of teaching-that informality. The fact that she never lectured. She raised a question and then invited the student to think about it, to respond to it-to answer it. Not that there was a correct answer, but what were some of the approaches to answering this particular question. It was a whole new way.
>
> My college education was almost entirely lectures in large classes, and we just listened and took notes and tried to remember. That was about it, but this was a whole new invitation to think approach, which I'd never met before. Certainly not in my college days, and it was intriguing to me. It was exciting ...
>
> Beyer, 9/29/78, pp. 43-44.

The following section will further analyze what this "method of teaching," this type of teaching that was different really was: "teaching like that."

Pedagogical Aspects

The first pedagogical aspect fostered in this type of teaching [*different*] was the way in which knowledge was framed and constructed by the faculty of Bank Street. It departed from ways in which knowledge had been conveyed to the teacher preparation program students in most of their school and college years. Before Bank Street, the form of teaching most students had experienced was didactic in large lecture settings. Knowledge in these lectures had a mimetic dimension. Jackson (1986) distinguishes between two traditions of teaching: mimetic and transformative. The first '...gives central place to the transmission of factual and procedural knowledge from one person to another, through an essentially imitative process" (p. 117). Most of the exposure to teaching that students had prior to Bank Street was rather mimetic. In contrast, the transformative tradition in teaching aims at "...a transformation of one kind or another in the person being taught--a qualitative change often of dramatic proportion, a metamorphosis, so to speak" (p. 121). This tradition better suits Bank [*Reason was b/c*] Street teaching since the focus of learning, the center, was the development of the prospective teacher as both a person and a professional. This is not to say that at Bank Street there wasn't room also for some mimetic teaching. However, as students confirm, most of the teaching was different from what was experienced before. According to a Bank Street faculty, this mimetic mode of teaching [*(Schools before Bank St.)*] did not provide the arena to engage in a larger conversation within the discipline, not to mention with anyone else in the class (Smith, 8/25/75). Thus, in contrast to the common teaching experiences to which students were exposed during their previous college years, the Bank Street program provided a different model of teaching. Referring to Lucy Sprague Mitchell, a student said:

> [*" student quote*]
> She made me feel there was a whole portion of learning and living that I'd never known about before, and that's a pretty exciting thing when you are still in your twenties and find out that there are other ways to think and to do, so that was pretty exciting.... She impressed you with her enthusiastic approach to thinking about any problems, whether it was the traffic that passed around your street, or the topographical aspect of New Jersey. That's where I was living at the time, and I learned a lot about that, which I never expected to learn.
>
> Beyer, 9/29/78, pp. 44-45.

Feeling and understanding were stressed as objectives of good teaching. A student said that they got from Mitchell: "that children need to know and feel directly the things.... this was part of the teacher's role: to help the child relate to things in such a way that he begins to have a feeling, an understanding" (Labowitz, 8/8/75, p. 11). Furthermore, if some of these students were to teach children the subject matter they were learning, solely lecturing would have limited access to knowledge and eventually limiting the possibilities of growing in understanding the complexities, nuances, structures, and relationships of the subject matter. It is not the argument that it is the function of every course of study at every level to expose and engage students in the debate over knowledge constitution within the discipline of study. The argument is for the need of a space to discuss, question, or challenge the text or the lecture or the experience. Faculty at Bank Street acted upon it.

Understanding was enhanced by providing students of teaching with intellectual tools to engage in critical thinking because the future teacher would be in a better position to be able to teach and build connections between children and the subject matter at hand (being it block building, social studies, or acting a play). These intellectual tools are ways of looking at situations, experiences, information, and arguments that try to unveil and challenge underlying assumptions, revise ideas, test them, and think of different and multiple possible ways of analyzing, explaining, and interpreting. A way of starting to think about subject matter connections was done through assignment that incorporated explorations and inquiry: For example, a student recalls that,

> We went to a corner, 7th Ave. & 14th St., come back and tell what we saw. Not only saw many trucks, auto, but where could they be coming from, going, why? What they carried. You realized bananas must come from some place and had to be transported through this particular street so people could eat these bananas which were being raised somewhere else. You had the total global picture there on 7th Ave. It stretched my mind. I've been traveling ever since then. I'd traveled before, but with that in mind, traveling has been much more important for me. Not only showcase of place, but people within it.
>
> Kandell, 9/15/75, p. 3.

A central element in learning to teach was for the prospective teachers to become aware of the ways in which instructors taught them. In addition, it was important to look closely at teaching as a subject matter to be studied. In other words, a dominant perspective was that in order to learn to teach "like that," it was necessary that students would experience "teaching like that."

Students of teaching at Bank Street learned by engaging with ideas, by testing different arguments, by challenging each other, by being challenged in a safe, caring, respectful, and above all a trusting environment. Students of teaching also learned from encountering structured experiences, from systematic inquiry, from a deep engagement with the activity of teaching children, and from thinking, analyzing and reflecting about the nature and effects of these experiences.

In addition to the purpose of becoming cognizant about subject matter, it was also the purpose to be cognizant about the learning experience. The idea of realizing learning, of becoming aware that learning was happening, of becoming aware of the process of building of connections, helped the students to differentiate between being provided with some information and being able to understand. A student stated:

> As I recall, our very first assignment was to go out on a street corner, close your eyes... and just listen and smell, and react to what was going on. At first we felt very silly doing these things, but pretty soon, when we understood the purpose and the relationship of this to the children's experience, we thoroughly enjoyed doing it.
>
> Killan, 2/20/76, pp. 3-4.

Therefore, to be able to "teach like that," students of teaching not just had to understand the subject matter, but also had to be aware and systematic about the processes by which knowledge had been conveyed to them. For example, an internal document that explained some of the meanings of the experience of art learning, stated that:

> The assumption is that only as the teacher herself has had the opportunity to develop beginning competence and to sense the satisfactions and release of such experience in her own life is she competent to understand the meaning which the arts may have for the developing life of a child. Only then is she prepared to appreciate, to say nothing of guide, the creative processes of the child. Thus, the prospective teacher not only enriches her own experience but also comes to understand how such experiences may best be used with children.
>
> Outline, 1937, p. 14.

[The difference in the type of experiences that students at Bank Street talked about, lay in the ways in which they were taught, which invited to think, to challenge, to make connections, to become passionate about teaching and learning] The passion was contagious, the faculty were also passionate in their own teaching. Referring to Lucy Sprague Mitchell, a student said: "She had a very animated face, and spoke with a great deal of animation about whatever it was that she was discussing" (Beyer, 9/29/78, p. 44). This pedagogical aspect at Bank Street was not only in terms of loving to work with people or loving children. The passion is also manifested in the loving of the subjects taught. Lucy Sprague Mitchell had a passion for writing, had a passion for geography: "She made geography something that was not just in the book and flat, but it was filled with people and there were contours and action" (Beyer, 9/29/75, p. 45). Another student reinforced this characteristic of Lucy's teaching: "I mean, she had a passion for children's development, but an equal passion for earth forces, and this entered her conversation constantly..." (Killan, 2/20/76, p. 8). These passions were also grounded in the validation of emotions as an important component of learning: "...the awareness that kids are not just mind and body, and that the educational process is not simply an intellectual process, but that the emotions need to be very deeply involved" (Smith, 8/25/75, p. 41). In turn, passion and emotion also drives curiosity and promotes discovery, enthusiasm for further learning, and constant engagement.

However, this engagement was nurtured because of a pedagogy that fostered intellectual respect. The teaching that Lucy Sprague Mitchell advocated and advanced grew out of intellectual respect, which prevented her from imposing her ideas on her students. She was truly interested in understanding her students' ideas and wonderment. She didn't press or intimidate her students to guess what she was thinking and to guess what was the right way of thinking. She made sure that students knew her thinking. She wanted to be challenged and to challenge. She wanted her students to articulate sensible arguments. Because of her respect she was also honest, which is a central component of building a trusting relationship. According to one of her students:

> At the dinner table she was exactly the same. This was Lucy. Pretty
> opinionated. She invited you to think, but she usually let you know
> what she thought before you were finished. Not that she expected
> you to join her. Or necessarily accept her thoughts, but she stated
> them clearly. You could choose. You were not bulldozed into

thinking what Lucy thought was right.

Beyer, 9/29/78, p. 44.

Yet, it was expected to be systematic and her pedagogy aimed at creating the habit of looking close at situations and children, at possible alternative explanations, at assessing implications, and at becoming an element that would inform decisions in everyday teaching. In order to make informed decisions about curriculum and about teaching, students had to learn to assess and to identify children's interests and learning. For instance a student referring to how they did assessment with Jessie Stanton, who taught curriculum classes, said:

> You kept track each day--this was a nine by twelve piece of paper-- manila paper, I think it was. You made this little chart, and you wrote down for each day the children's activities that sort of dominated: Block play, painting clay, outdoor...all of these things that they would be the actors in their play. Then you kept track of discussion on these days, the topics of discussion, the books or stories that were read, any trips that were taken, and these were divided into categories: Domestic, transportation, farm...oh, I can't really recall all of them. Each category had a color, so that you'd underline all of the farm activities, and then you saw to what extent they'd been followed by discussion or with stories, so that the relatedness of input to outflow was clearly quite dramatic, and very visual... At least, if you began to get clues of interest in farm activities, then, by what the children were playing, in the block, for instance, you might follow it up with a story, or with a discussion, or with a trip. So every week she'd go over this chart with you and see to what extent you were following through, or you were getting clues, or what omissions there were. She'd help. It wasn't in a critical sense, but in a helping mood to see what was going on.
>
> Beyer, 9/29/78, p. 22.

The above description highlights several interesting aspects of the meaning of inquiry and assessment. First, it is clear that an essential element was to see if children learned, and, in consequence, how to design and redesign the environment. Second, it helped the prospective teacher to learn more about the children in their particular classroom, the children styles, their ways of making sense, the patterns that would help individualize needs. Third, it invited to make larger connections between some patterns in the micro-culture of the classroom and the context of the school. Finally, it helps the prospective teacher to see themselves as teachers in relation to children.

Furthermore, the way in which students were learning inquiry shows a relaxed and non-threatening relationship with the supervisor-teacher. A student-teacher, who many years after her experience became a faculty member, summarized it this way:

> We had been encouraged, of course, in our work as students at Bank Street, to write down things, carrying little pads in our pockets, and not let the children's words escape us, write up the things we saw that we thought were important, we wanted to remember, that were important in understanding children. We were constantly writing.
>
> Lewis, 3/26/75, pp. 22-23.

Inquiry provided opportunities to problematize, to question, and to unveil underlying assumptions, and it was a form of research that was meaningful for classroom teaching. Then, the idea was to focus the power of a well informed and thoughtful teacher in ways that will have also an effect on how to treat their students and what type of relations they will foster in their classrooms. According to a faculty member:

> Teachers and students really need to be a cooperating link. I know that isn't a very apt expression, but teachers are not something up here and students down here. Teachers may have had somewhat more experience and lived a few years longer, but the educational process is a sharing of experiences, an inter-active process. You needed to have an open street between the two so that you could easily communicate with each other.
>
> Smith, 8/25/75, p. 45.

The student could not be solely seen as an individual entity. The child was in a social context and the child was in the context of the small community that the classroom represents. What was valued and what was not valued started to establish the learning of social norms. The same faculty member (Smith, 8/25/75, p. 59) reflected that:

> When I think back occasionally to the crime it was to whisper in school, it suggests the contrast. I think the social interaction of the kids in school is another one of the important dimensions of the educational philosophy. Children have a lot to learn from and contribute to each other and you can't just depend on it as a one way street between the teacher and the student.

Faculty emphasized the connection and meaning of what was discussed and explored in their classes with the ways in which children might make sense of these ideas. This influenced in meaningful ways the structuring of an environment to create situations for children learning. Therefore, stories about children become another teaching tool. During class students at Bank Street will volunteer anecdotes and stories that they had experienced in classrooms working with children. Faculty, in turn guided the conversation to make important connections with larger ideas. Each story was treated as a potential case for further analysis, discussion and learning. As a student recalls,

> Of course, she always loved hearing the stories about the children and their comments, and she made awfully good use of them. We went in spring to see the little new-born lambs. This little lamb was nursing its mother, wiggling its tail like mad and everyone was touching it. Jessie was with us. She said, 'What do you suppose it's doing?' there was absolute silence, nobody knew. And then this little tiny boy said, 'Well, he's tickling his mother.' She was very −'Well, may-be he is. Maybe something else is happening.' One little guy spoke up and said, 'I know! He's getting gasoline!' Jessie just loved that. She just thought that was marvelous. And she used that to show the confusion.
>
> Beyer, 9/29/78, p. 23.

Stories were also used to illustrate the impact of the context of the children's life on the classroom's life. It was meant also to help the prospective teachers to understand how to build connections according to the children's development.

> A typical story is of a child down at the Little Red School House, who built a farm. On the first floor he had the chickens, and on the second floor the cows, and on the third floor the horses, all the way up to the roof ... and the elevator man was the farmer.
>
> Killan, 9/29/78, p. 23.

The use of the above story in teaching teachers illustrates the nature of "teaching like that" at Bank Street. It immersed the student in thinking about children's ways of making sense of their experiences. It furthered the analysis of classroom environments to move the child beyond their actual experience. It considered the outside context that conditioned what the child brought to this relationship.

The pedagogy of teacher education in this case fostered an array of aspects that enabled learning about the self, learning about the world, learning about children, and learning to teach (Teacher Education Curriculum, 1938). It made their experience a subject matter of study, grounding it in an inquiry oriented approach, with an adventurous disposition, passion, and intellectual engagement.

Student-Teacher Knowledge of Subject Matter

The program at Bank Street was built on the assumption that the prior education of the student-teacher provided knowledge of subject matter. At Bank Street subject matter knowledge was not a topic or a dimension of learning. Perhaps, the assumption is a result of the students' college background. Having attended prestigious liberal arts and women colleges provided some assurance that students knew the subject matter they were to teach. This was a problematic issue because it was very uncertain that prospective teachers who completed an undergraduate degree understood the ways in which knowledge was conceptualized, constructed, and validated in different disciplines.

Also, very little attention was paid to the teaching of subject matter in a balanced manner. For instance, students at Bank Street gained a systematic understanding in the teaching of social studies. They learned to construct and validate geographical knowledge and to relate it to children in meaningful ways. However, the same cannot be certain about the teaching of mathematics. The best that can be said for this subject is the sophistication in the use of blocks. They were important in the school curriculum mainly for pre-school and kindergarten children and were used among other things for pre-math concept development like learning about size and shapes. Yet, there was no systematic learning of what they called "the tool subjects" in the Bank Street program. Student teachers learned a lot about children and learned a lot about experimenting and exploring. However, knowing children well and knowing the subject matter well, and even knowing how to be an experimental teacher, does not guarantee knowing how to build a learning community in every subject area. On the other hand, the view of the teacher as a naturalist, as a scholar, as a citizen, and as a researcher, provided the possibility of lifelong learning for the student-teacher by also fostering an experimental and adventurous disposition, open-minded, and a critical perspective, which were necessary for what Bank Street envisioned.

CHAPTER SIX

The Conceptual Base
of Teacher Education

The conceptual base of teacher education for Bank Street during these early years of the institution was rather broad in scope and had a direct, intrinsic, connection between what they believed to be a curriculum for a child and, parallel to it, a curriculum to prepare teachers. For a child, the curriculum referred to all the experiences of the child in and out of school. The argument was that in order to provide an educative environment in school, the school had to take into account the child as a whole. All the aspects of a child's development, then, became the concern of the Bank Street concept of curriculum. Furthermore, since these developments also occurred outside the school setting, the teacher had to think of the context and background of the child's life when designing the learning environment and the activities: "Curriculum is used here to refer to the sum total of the child's experience both inside the school and outside since the school must take in the whole life of the child in determining its educational program" (Outline, 1937, p. 13).

The experiences at the school setting, thus, build upon the child's prior experiences in and out of the school. But it is not just for purposes of providing a safe and validating environment, it means, as Dewey (1938) also suggested, to move beyond these prior experiences: "The belief that all genuine education comes about through experience does not mean that all experiences are genuinely or equally educative" (p. 25). This means to provide learning opportunities that probably cannot happen in other environments but in the school. The teacher should provide an educative experience by connecting the excitement and adventure of learning the world with the validation and context of the child's environment.

> It was more a matter of expressing what they experienced in order
> to understand it in the intellectual sense... It wasn't that they
> expressed their feelings in an art form and said this really to
> somebody else in the same way. It was: See a train, and make a
> picture of a train that this is the whistle and this is the smoke stack,
> and this is the rear car, and shows that you really, clearly see that
> car and know how a train operates, and then, the next thing is:
> Where is the train going? That's a little different from expressing
> anger or hatred or love or whatever it is you might express in an art
> form.
>
> Labowitz, 8/8/75, p. 12.

The curriculum of teacher preparation at Bank Street was conceptualized
and designed upon the principles of what they believed to be a student-
centered curriculum. In this case, it was a curriculum that built upon the life
experiences of a particular group of selected students, that was shaped upon
the cultural capital (or cultural property) of these students, and upon the
assumptions about the students' liberal education background (Bourdieu,
1977; Labaree, 1988). The curriculum aimed at moving prospective teachers
beyond their prior experiences to install a set of habits built upon a carefully
designed set of learning opportunities. "Unless experience is so conceived
that the result is a plan for deciding upon subject-matter, upon methods of
instruction and discipline, and upon material equipment and social
organization of the school, it is wholly in the air" (Dewey, 1938, p. 28). This
means engaging the student in both a process of validation and a process of
critique and reassessment in relation to a body of knowledge.

These ideas about curriculum were influenced by Dewey's idea of
"..continuous reconstruction, moving from the child's (student) present
experience out into that represented by the organized bodies of truth that we
call studies...they present this...in some organized and systematized way--
that is, as reflectively formulated" (Dewey, 1902/1964, pp. 344-345).

Dewey's influence in the views on curriculum is most evident in the
required list of readings in the class on "Curriculum." As shown in the
syllabus attached to a letter sent by Randolph Smith on April 3, 1937, in this
class, which lasted 15 meetings of 2 hrs., out of 11 required readings, five
were Dewey's writings. Interestingly, some of these readings were available
to Bank Street faculty and students before their publication. From Dewey, it
was required to read (a) "The child and the curriculum," (b) "Democracy and
education," (c) "Schools of tomorrow," (d) "Art as experience," and (e)
"Experience and education."

Thus, the conceptual base for this view of curriculum is progressive, and it has an impact on the role of the teacher and on good teaching, which fostered an experimental, inquiry oriented, and child-centered practice, but with a strong social commitment. In terms of curriculum for teacher preparation, the above conceptual base translates as follows:

> You couldn't have a list of courses and say the students learn. That was really the basic idea: That some of the learning had to follow a course that it was generated from the students' experience, not from a planned curriculum. You had a planned curriculum, but that wasn't enough.
>
> Biber, 8/13/75, p. 15.

[The label "student-teacher centered curriculum" captures the perspective that the focus of teacher education was the preparation and growth of the prospective teacher as a person and as a professional generating a program that responds to the students' needs and developments] This characterization is important because it privileges the student as a knower and as a constructor of meaning, rather than privileging a body of knowledge generated in isolation from the student. The learning occurs, in this view, when the students' needs are met, when the students gain ownership over the knowledge, and when students make knowledge theirs. Thus, the curriculum provides a framework and an elaborated environment to nurture the student growth, yet it is flexible and uncertain since knowledge is constructed and explored rather than handed. [Bank Street curriculum provided environments that nurtured learning about teaching not only through courses, but also through field experiences] These experiences ranged from occasional field trips and art production, to intense practice in schools with children and with teachers.]

> The notion of learning at firsthand often means that it gets incorporated a bit better. Also, of course, the notion that the educational process is a reactive one and that it's not only intake but it's also outgo. So art and shop and music and drama and everything else is an essential part of the learning process; in other words, the digestive apparatus has to work with the intellectual data. You have to use all five senses, not just your eyesight.
>
> Smith, 8/25/75, p. 47.

This perspective recognized that learning could be more powerful when based on a combination of firsthand experiences and responsibilities. These experiences, however, have to be organized in a such way that they provide an educational meaning. If Dewey's premises about the nature of the experience and about the relationship between practice and theory were to be incorporated in the curriculum, it meant that these firsthand experiences had to be carefully scrutinized and systematically evaluated by both student-teachers and faculty. Thus, the curriculum for prospective teachers considered practice-teaching as an integrated component to the more formally organized course work: "...as simultaneous experiences which from the beginning should proceed along together with constant reciprocal interaction, each continually dependent upon the other, each continually contributing to the other" (Outline, 1937, p. 7).

It is important to notice that practice-teaching was a central component of the curriculum from the very beginning of the year. The developmentalist influence was present here in terms of adding responsibilities as the student grew in understanding, meanings, and needs.

The Connection of Theory and Practice at Bank Street

Although the course work of the curriculum extensively covered and made students aware of

> ...child development and child psychology, of the salient emphases
> in contemporary educational philosophy and psychology, of the
> outstanding developments in curriculum content, curriculum
> planning, special methods, and classroom organization, and of the
> role of the teacher and the school in contemporary society, it
> should not be assumed that the course program represents the
> distinction between theory and practice. On the contrary the
> curriculum is conceived as a single unified pedagogical whole with
> course content richly illustrated, challenged and verified constantly
> by direct appeal to the evidence of children and the classroom.
>
> Outline, 1937, p. 11.

The organization of the curriculum with its ongoing interchange of course and classroom experience was planned to strengthen the relation between theory and practice. Theories that can't be examined or tested in terms of their effects in classroom life, school realities, and child growth, or practices that have no theoretical framework were both perceived to be at least unfitted for teaching consideration.

The centrality of extensive and intensive field experiences in the curriculum is due to the assumption that nothing "can take the place of extensive, intimate, first-hand student contact with children of the particular age levels which the teacher expects to teach" (Outline, 1937, p. 4). [The curriculum was organized to provide a maximum of opportunity to learn from the experiences in classrooms with children and with skilled teachers.] Another advantage of an extensive and intensive field experience is the learning of the school life and of the philosophies, ideas, and perspectives of the particular school. The schools were private progressive and experimental. [The close connection with the school allowed the student to become part of its community and also to gain understanding about the procedures and teaching techniques] Through daily work with outstanding teachers,

> Students see the inside workings of a school, observe and participate in the day to day responsibilities of the teacher, obtain experience in the investigation and organization of curriculum content and source materials, share in the development and execution of curriculum plans. They assume increasing responsibility for special aspects of the program such as the conduct of environment field trips, the leadership of group discussions, the case study of individual children, the supervision of particular personal or group projects. The individual guidance and instruction of children in special need of assistance, care of physical health and recreation, the study and development of improved teaching methods to suit the special needs of both individual children and the group as a whole are all contained within the gamut of their experience.
>
> Teacher Education Curriculum, 1938, pp. 4-5.

Student-teachers experienced the teacher's responsibility. Being for four days a week in schools, the students learned about the uncertainties and complexities of practical problems. Students might have different inclinations and personal capacities to teach children of different ages and characteristics. Then, it was necessary to help students find their own preferences and to provide different experiences that might enhance the understanding of childhood. Thus, there were opportunities to be placed in at least two or more classrooms during the year. Further, there were visits to other school buildings. These visits also served to compare and learn from the different perspectives, practices, and contexts.

The placement of the student in a school setting for the practice-teaching component of the program was made in consultation with the student. The process of consultation and decision included an analysis of the student's interests and experiences. It included an evaluation of qualifications to match a student for work with a particular age level rather than another. Placements were made with the understanding that there may be a need for change at different times during the year because of particular needs of the student. These needs, for example, could be a change of preference to work with a certain age group or the need to practice in a classroom with a different group of children or a different teacher.

An enormous part of the value of the practice-teaching experience depended on the success of the placement decision. This decision assumed two factors: (a) the selection of students to the program; (b) a group of teachers in each school who were able to guide and mentor the development of the student-teachers and who were committed to invest the time and energy for the success of this relationship. Thus, the selection of this group of teachers and the relationships between these teachers and Bank Street was an essential link of the program. Although there is no available evidence on the selection process of the teacher, the fact that these teachers taught at the cooperating schools ensured that there was a coherence of vision about teaching and learning and about the dispositions and the role of the teacher. The cooperating schools shared the commitments of Bank Street to prepare progressive teachers who will teach in progressive schools since they not only helped to form the CST, but also some of the directors had an active role teaching at the CST. The relationship between the classroom teacher and the student-teacher involved mentoring and collegiality. However, there was no data available about the nature of these relationships between the cooperating teacher and the student teacher. Further, there was no evidence that the teachers did not receive any type of support from Bank Street faculty nor that they had regular meetings or study groups to work on their practices as mentors. These cooperating schools hired many graduates of Bank Street. By 1937, the cooperating schools where students were placed were The Little Red School House, The Harriet Johnson Nursery School, and The Rosemary Junior School, Greenwich, Connecticut, which were well known for their experimental approach to education (Winsor, 1973).

A basic assumption to this program was that the preparation of teachers had to offer an array of educational opportunities. This program was not a recipe of ideas to be implemented mechanically by teachers once they had their own classrooms. It was conceived to prepare the future teacher as an independent thinker. The curriculum provided a blend of a developmentalist approach with Dewey's experientialism and with social reconstructionism. The program had a curriculum that intertwined practice-teaching, systematic inquiry, field trips, artistic exposure, course content, and analysis in order to cover the different knowledge dimensions necessary for successful teaching.

In turn, these conceptual perspectives shaped the way in which knowledge, curriculum, all the experiences including the practice areas, and teaching as a subject matter, were thought, organized, and enacted to provide a structured educative experience. These perspectives are organized here as curricular elements, learning community, and the coherence of the program.

Programmatic Elements

The following discussion of programmatic elements that framed teacher education at Bank Street includes curricular elements, learning community, and coherence.

Curricular Elements

[Curricular elements refer to the aspects of the program that focus on knowledge] and they encompass not just the courses of study but the whole learning experience. At Bank Street, outcomes and learning dimensions juxtaposed over the traditional fragmentation of knowledge associated with only one particular class. As shown in Chapters IV and V, knowledge was not conceptualized as a decontextualized piece of information outside the realm of the student as a knower. On the contrary, knowledge and knower were intrinsically connected, and this curricular approach focused on the learner needs as well.

The first element is what I labeled "curriculum beyond the confines of the course." An interesting aspect of the Bank Street curriculum was its emphasis on the dimensions of learning to teach across courses rather than on the courses as independent units of knowledge. It meant that by having the four dimensions (self, world, child, school), the knowledge was seen as connected. Furthermore, the four dimensions enhanced the conceptualization of knowledge for teaching. Dimensions such as learning about the self and about the world were as important to the program curriculum as learning about children or about school work.

While often courses fragment bites of information and domains of understanding, by having certain common strands throughout the coursework and the field teaching experiences the curriculum at Bank Street was more integrated. The advantage was to help the student grow in the different dimensions throughout all of the experiences. Some experiences had more emphasis on some domains than others. However, there were two lines of emphasis in such an approach. One was the importance of the processes as outcomes, since the combination of domains of learning also incorporated the notion of making the learning part of the subject matter of study. Second, the shared vision of accomplishing a common set of outcomes is enacted throughout the different experiences. Taking a course on child development didn't mean to disconnect this area of understanding and expertise from other courses of study, from the field experiences, and also to isolate this area of knowledge from the other domains (the self, the school, or the world). On the contrary, the content and the teaching of such a course contributed to a better understanding and growth on all of the other domains.

The second aspect of these curricular elements is that the "curriculum focuses on students' development." The idea that certain contents and certain experiences should happen at certain appropriate times according to the development of student-teacher needs, and understanding is different from establishing a number of courses to be taken without any criteria of order and connection. In addition, an important element in this approach was the parallel experience of student teaching with the coursework.

Coursework was not organized to prepare the student for student-teaching, but for support and shape of the student-teaching experience--it was not just a response to the field experience but a framework of reference and a builder of the experience. This approach is different, but not in contradiction, from the common curriculum approach in which there is a need for a hierarchical understanding of content. The freshness of this perspective was on the focus. The learner of teaching became the focus of how the content and experiences got organized. The concerns, motivations, tensions, wonderment, surprises, interests, questions, and growth that experienced student-teachers during their exposure to the field experiences became the central process that organized the curriculum. Rather than preparing for a future field experience, the field experience was used as the medium to determine the type of support, knowledge, and practices, in which the student-teacher was engaged. This requires a systematic understanding of the student teacher learning processes. This also implies some assumptions about stages by which student teacher experiences get organized. While the program responded to individual student needs, the program couldn't fit all the different personal characteristics and concerns. Bank Street structured the program according to larger patterns of needs. This was an accommodation of experiences and course work and organized content. Initially, for the first seven years of existence of this program, this accommodation also included a course on personality that served as an advisory mechanism to meet individual developments in the context of a group support. By the end of the 1930s, based on this original course, Bank Street developed the advisory approach, which organized ongoing regular sessions with groups of about six students to address similar issues as the ones in the personality class, but with better opportunity to participate and support each other.

The connections among and between class experiences departed from seeing the program as an accumulation of classes. In this perspective, there should be a sequence, and there should be a close connection with the learning processes of the student teachers in relation not just to content but to the practice. Furthermore, the Bank Street "approach" also consisted of closer attention to individual differences. Structured spaces, such as seminars where the focus of the course was the student-teacher development and not necessarily a focus only on issues of teaching and learning in the classroom, was created. Thus, for pedagogical and personal learning, there was a connected structured seminar.

The implication of developmental, experimental, experiential, and pragmatic approaches is that the field experience component of learning to teach, the practice teaching provides also a testing arena where consequences can be evaluated and scrutinized, because it goes parallel and is connected with the course work,. This means that the practice teaching is far longer (in Bank Street it lasted one year) than the common 12 or 15 weeks of student teaching as a culminating experience.

Learning Community

Another element of the experience at CST was the building of a learning community. Learning community in this context means the experiences, objectives, needs, intentions, interests, motivations that a group shares in order to have educative situations where learning takes place in a safe, caring, trusted, and challenging environment. A learning community as a concept has a double meaning because community can be learned and because learning is a communal enterprise (Schwab, 1976). Furthermore, I argue that a learning community as in the Bank Street case encompasses learning in community, which includes a constructivist view of learning with and from one another, building and relying on each other, intellectual challenges, and collaboration and growth. It also embraces the aspects of learning to live in a community by exploring the limitations and potential of individual and group rights and duties, respect, trust, and dependency. In addition, it is connected, not divorced from, the local community, as demonstrated not only in the curricular experiences, but also in the aspects of learning the world. Therefore, CST built this learning community within the social realm, learning to be a community and about community, and also within the academic discourse realm, having a learning community where ideas and experiences were constructed. These realms helped to build a culture of the institution that transcended as part of the ethos about what later became Bank Street.

Even though the group had some differences in terms of age, lifestyles, or life experiences, there was commonality in terms of cultural and socio-economic background. An element that caused the group cohesiveness in social terms was the organization of the course-work in a concentrated schedule. The intensity of work from Thursday evening until Saturday evenings provoked a situation of being in the same place at the same time for a long and excruciating period. Although sometimes too much time together creates friction, a shared status as students, the intensity of the schedule and activities, and the attractiveness and excitement of the material and class content in most cases, created a sense of common purpose. The organization of the program helped on getting to know each other in and out of class. In turn, this translated, in most cases, into respect and trust.

As mentioned above, the pedagogy fostered in the program helped in the building of the learning community. The way of communicating, of talking through different personal and social issues, the ways of listening, and the ways of dealing with personal and social conflict in and out of the group was certainly shaped by the conversations in class. Events like field trips, the long trip, dancing, and singing together, helped in the process of group crystallization. Group formation is the growing cohesiveness and sense of commonality, caring for each other, and a sense of mission and togetherness that occurs when people who share some experiences, ideas, and commitments undergo group and individual processes and interactions. This crystallization can become a powerful element on building a learning community.

This process of group formation was also achieved by the "tea" events. Several formal and informal meetings took place in the library where tea and fine cookies were served in porcelain sets. The library was a very warm and cozy place that provided a sense of intimacy. This example of the "tea" events suggests that the creation of informal spaces within the structure of the program may be powerful for building community. These tea events also served as an occasion for faculty to talk with students in less formal and hierarchical ways. This ambiance of camaraderie served the purpose of the learning community because of its profound social element.

Another "informal" experience suggests the need for social interactions in the building of community. Several students used to sleep overnight at 69 Bank Street, the house of the CST, and the nursery school. This was because of either lack of resources or because of a sense for adventure, There were no comfortable facilities, and certainly there was no city habilitation for such a function of the building. Nevertheless, faculty didn't object and students took the risk of staying over. This staying together in the same place added a level of intimacy to the whole experience to some of the students. In addition, it contributed the sense of ownership over the physical place and the sense of obligation towards the institution. The building of a learning community through formal and informal experiences responded to the concept that learning and knowledge construction occur in safe, respectful, and trusting social contexts. Experiencing a learning community was important if the future teachers were to value it as an important context for their own future teaching of children. If teachers were to foster learning communities in their classrooms, they had to experience what it was like to learn in such a community themselves.

Coherence

Coherence refers to a logical and consistent connection of elements. Furthermore, it refers to the integration of diverse elements, perspectives, and values. Program coherence encompasses three different facets: (a) coherence in content; (b) coherence between the course-work and field experiences; and (c) continuity and sustainability of coherence between what was learned in the program and the settings or schools where graduates of the program performed their professional activities.

The first facet is "coherence in content." In this context, coherence in content refers to a set of connected and integrated dispositions, of reflective habits, of analytic and critical views, and of multiple perspectives, with respect to learning about teaching in the program content and experiences. It is not one message repeated several times by different people. It is a consistent message about the roles and responsibilities of teaching and to a broad scope of perspectives in relation to the professional activity. In the case of the CST, we have certain perspectives that repeat and reinforce each other, and we have examples of different emphases, angles, and arguments about the whole idea of educating. Coherence can be seen as the metaphor of the diamond that depending on the position, the angle, and the light, the colors and forms seen will vary (Buchmann & Floden, 1990). Similarly in the case of CST, the content provides a different conversation within the framework of an experimental and progressive view of schooling and education. Further, and in spite of the different experiences and expertise of the faculty, there was coordination in terms of looking and thinking about each other's content and pedagogy. This means that there was an effort to provide a coherent experience through the curriculum and the practices provided to each student.

A second facet of programmatic coherence is that between coursework and field-experience. This is the coordination of the relationship between what students of teaching learned in the coursework and what they observed and experienced in their field placements. The sort of views about teaching and learning that they explored and analyzed in their course-work was reinforced by the practices that they were exposed to during their field experiences. The aim of providing a meaningful environment for learning through the practices that were advocated at the CST, was in solid presence at the classrooms where CST students were placed.

Furthermore, the general school culture and commitments were coherent with the views advocated at the CST. This was a very important piece of teacher preparation for two reasons. First, it was relevant because it carries the message that "it could be done," that the ideas and concepts could be practiced, and that a close and systematic scrutiny of these practices might rebuild theory. Second, it was important because not just the possibility of nurturing and practicing in a supportive environment in terms of training was real, but also and fundamentally, it provided the possibility to be exposed to models of practice to student-teachers that were not exposed to these types of teaching in their own schooling.

The models to what these students of teaching were exposed in their own school experience was rather the focus of critique of these pedagogical and curricular perspectives. It could have been quite difficult to expose only theoretically the ideas of experimentalism and progressivism in teaching. The coherent element of the field experience provided models to break from their own prior experiences. Thus, the challenge to a coherent teaching was in the evaluation of its consequences. This meant not just to engage with ideas, but also to enact practice and to examine its consequences.

The third facet of coherence is that of "continuity and sustainability" between the ideas and practices learned during their teacher preparation at CST with the future work setting. Because of the special market demands from private progressive schools, most of the graduates of CST secured jobs and were recruited by schools that shared the ideas, culture, and perspectives of experimentalism and progressivism in classroom and school life. In a sense then one of the difficulties that some graduates of teacher education may face is that of having to deny their own learning (Zeichner & Gore, 1990). Therefore, there is some re-learning required that focuses solely on mere technicalities as the new teachers try to conform to the culture and politics of the institution (Feiman-Nemser & Floden, 1986). However, for graduates of CST the case was different. Their teaching was not isolated, learning from experience was systematic, and the curriculum and pedagogies validated during their teacher preparation were valued, nurtured, encouraged, and supported in the school settings where they got jobs. It was a very different way of being a novice teacher. Teachers who thought and taught this brand of progressivism needed institutional structures and cultures that sustained and nurtured their practices and their views.

CHAPTER SEVEN

Institutional Organization

This chapter will describe and analyze what is special and salient about Bank Street in terms of organization and arrangements: institutional independence of Bank Street, the functions of the different parts and individuals, the finances, and the faculty background. Also, this section will cover characteristics of the Cooperating Schools and their relationship with Bank Street as an institution, the placement of students, the nature of the student body, the recruitment strategies, the admissions process, and the job market for graduates of the program.

The teacher education program was one of the divisions of the Bank Street Schools (a new name that replaced the Bureau for Educational Experiments when the organization moved to its new location at 69 Bank Street, New York, in 1931). The other divisions were (a) the Research Division which continued part of the work of the former Bureau of Educational Experiments headed by Barbara Biber at the time of moving, (b) the Nursery School headed by Harriet Johnson and after her death by Jessie Stanton, and (c) a publications division that did not fully materialize until the creation of the Writers' Workshops in the late 1930s.

One central pattern in the history of teacher education has been the problem of ownership over their programs and the competition with faculty in colleges of arts and sciences (Warren, 1985; Urban, 1990). However, Bank Street was not part of any other university or college and did not have programs in other disciplines. Therefore, it did not have to deal and compete with arts and science faculty, deans, or a central administration. The institution did not offer a state validated credential until 1938. Nor did it initially provide a degree. It was not until 1937, when the agenda of the institution focused on trying to influence and change public schools, that a charter to prepare teachers was provided by the State of New York. In 1937, Bank Street decided to apply for a Charter to the State of New York. The purpose of the charter was to be able to provide students with a state teacher credential. The purpose was that Bank Street after its initial few years should continue to prepare experimental teachers not only for private schools but also for the public schools (R. Smith, 8/25/75). They also expected that a credential recognized by the state may validate Bank Street in the eyes of public schools in order to gain an entry to work with veteran teachers in New York schools, as Lucy Sprague Mitchell did a few years latter (Sprague Mitchell, 1951).

Its institutional independence allowed the teacher education program to be shaped by the beliefs and perspectives of its faculty. In short, faculty had ownership over the program in terms of deciding its policy directions, content and courses, field experiences, and relationships with schools and other institutions and individuals. It didn't need the approval of any external body.

Standard teacher education had been criticized because of its fragmented and intellectually poor curriculum, with easy classes, privileging quantity over quality. Part for the inadequacy of traditional teacher education programs lay on its institutional dependencies and on market pressures (Labaree, 1992; Urban, 1990; Warren, 1985). Compared with other institutions that prepared teachers, the CST was in a privileged situation from the organizational point of view.

First, standard teacher education programs were part of Colleges or Schools of Education where preparation of teachers was not the main commitment. Normal Schools lost their purpose by growing into institutions that by responding to market needs enhanced their curriculums, but where most students did not have an interest in teacher education classes (Altenbaugh & Underwood, 1990; Herbst, 1989; Labaree, 1993). At Bank Street the preparation of teachers was top priority in contrast to many colleges of education where teacher preparation was low status (Clifford & Guthrie, 1988).

Second, at CST, faculty "owned" the program in contrast to other teacher education programs where education faculty had to share with faculty from arts and sciences. Third, at Bank Street program changes and experimental implementations were easily discussed and approved, while in other places they had to be approved by different colleagues, senates, provosts, graduate schools, and frequently by State departments of education and also by the legislature.

Because of its small size, it was not difficult to change and to implement new elements in the program. The only commitment existed between the program and the cooperating schools. As mentioned before, some of the directors and some teachers from the cooperating schools taught classes and gave short lectures or workshops from time to time. Bank Street had a close connection with the New School for Social Research, which provided part of their facilities and faculty for some classes. For instance, in the first year of the program the class on child development was taught at the New School by a faculty of the New School (Barbara Biber, 8/13/75). In addition, Pearson taught the art class at the New School for several years.

The connection with the New School is not casual because Wesley Mitchell, husband of Lucy, was one of the founders and Alvin Johnson, the director of the New School, was on the Board of Trustees of what became the Bank Street School. W. Mitchell was a strong and active supporter of the New School since its conceptualization and foundation (Rutkoff & Scott, 1986). But there was also an ideological connection since the two institutions represented alternative opportunities to the way in which Universities functioned, taught, and established policies for research and academic freedom.

CST's institutional autonomy not only reinforced the sense of mission and coherence, it also left the program independent from the politics, bureaucratic processes, and dependency that constrained teacher education programs in other institutions.

Organization and Functions

Below is an organizational chart of the different entities and their hierarchies at Bank Street (Annual Report, 1934-1935).

Figure 3: Organizational Chart

Board of Trustees Working Council Executive Committee   Director Nursery School   Studies and Research   Publications   Cooperative School Central Staff Administrative Program/ General Secretary Educational Programs

At the top of this hierarchy is the Board of Trustees, and the Cooperative School is one of the four divisions. Following the chart there is a section in which the functions and responsibilities are explained.

Director

The CST's director (General Secretary) was Elizabeth Ross, and later, in 1935, it was Randolph Smith. Furthermore, there was a secretary and some administrative aids in addition to the faculty. Some faculty at CST had other responsibilities. For instance, besides teaching, Barbara Biber was doing research, Harriet Johnson directed the nursery school, and Lucy Sprague Mitchell served in the Board of Trustees, in the Working Council, and took responsibility in building relations with other institutions, doing fund-raising, and running projects like the writers workshop.

Board of Trustees

Bank Street had a Board of Trustees, which functioned as an advisory board by providing suggestions, ideas, recommendations, and by offering political and institutional connections. However, when the secretary recommended to amend the charter of the Bureau in order to give official recognition to the teacher education program, the minutes of a Board meeting, dated November 23rd, 1934, show unanimous approval of the motion with no record of discussion. Members also recommended potential new Board members. No records show conflict among the members of the board who seemed to be a good group of powerful and knowledgeable advisors like Wesley Mitchell, also a professor of economy at Columbia University, Alvin Johnson, an internationally known social scientist, the founder of the University in Exile, and the President of The New School for Social Research, F. Aydelotte, president of Swarthmore College, who was also the American Secretary for the Rhodes trustees and a board member of the Guggenheim Foundation, and educators such as W. Kilpatrick, professor at Teachers College, Columbia University (Catalogue, 1933-1934).

The Board owned the school property, acted on budget issues, advised on financial policy, and considered and evaluated educational reports. Prior trustees elected new members. The usual number of trustees was nine. Usually a member of the Nursery School and of the Cooperative School served on the Board. In addition, there were usually a member of the business community, a parent of children in the Nursery School, and educators.

Working Council

The CST program had a Working Council composed of faculty representatives, the director, and Lucy Sprague Mitchell. The Working Council provided educational guidance and decision making. It was the policy making and executive entity of the program. The Council also prepared the budget. Membership was decided by election of the faculty and candidates had to be active faculty with major responsibility at Bank Street (e.g., directing the Nursery School or the Research Division). The Working Council usually had nine members, with two serving as the Executive Committee. The Director of the Cooperative School usually served on the Executive Committee, which was appointed by the Chair of the Council with its approval.

Central Staff

The Central Staff had a Chair elected from within. The Central Staff elaborated educational and financial plans. It was also responsible for admissions, services to the community, organization of courses and studies, scheduling, and coordination with teaching staff. The Central Staff also appointed the faculty of the Cooperative School.

Administrative Program

The Administrative Program was a title for those employees responsible for care and use of the building and all the business details of the institution. There was a General Secretary and an Assistant elected by the Working Council. Their responsibilities included maintaining correspondence, publications, interviewing student applicants, placements of student-teachers, and all the logistics of the programs.

Educational Programs

The Working Council and the General Secretary shared responsibility for the teacher education program with the teaching staff of the program, the Directors of the Cooperating Schools, and with teachers in the schools.

Internal Relationships

The different organizational entities of the institutional structure at Bank Street seemed to collaborate and work in harmony during the 1930s. These relationships were also shaped by a sense of common mission and shared commitments. Furthermore, because of its progressive and democratic ideas about schooling, these same ideas were fostered in the administration of the institution.

> ...you needed to get together in a quasi-democratic group and thrash out your problems and work out the hoped-for solutions and that the people directly involved ought to have a chance to share with each other their thinking and planning.
>
> Smith, 8/25/75, p. 31.

Finances

Institutional independence carried a price in terms of resources and finances. The CST (and Bank Street Schools) always needed economic support from Board members and friends, and external fund raising was a frequent activity. For instance, Mrs. Mitchell and Miss Healy reported a meeting with Dr. Keppel of the Carnegie Foundation regarding an application for a grant. Furthermore, this meeting was mostly dedicated to identify fund raising strategies (Board of Trustees, 12/13/33). The Mitchells donated money to help maintain a balanced budget. In 1934 Mrs. Mitchell contributed $5,400.00 (Board of Trustees, 5/29/34).

The cost of studies at CST was high and the intensity and time of the program didn't allow the student to have a regular job during the year of practice-teaching since they had to be in the schools. For instance, for the 1933-1934 school year, the tuition was $350, but students were able to secure loans if necessary. For the same school year, of 32 full-time students, 22 paid full tuition, one student had a full scholarship, three students had partial scholarships, and eight students took loans from the Bank Street Loan Fund. A few part-time students took one or two classes and paid proportional tuition.

The program was expensive to run, although the salaries of faculty were low and many of the short lectures and/or courses were taught for free. Salaries of teachers in the program represented about 20% of the budget in 1932-1933, more than 25% for the following year, and about 25% for the year 1934-1935. Building expenses, another important item in the budget, ranged from 20% to 25% of the expenses. The highest cost was the administration, which included salaries for individuals working in these capacities. This item of the budget shows a steady increase from 25% of the expenses for the year 1932-1933, to 33% for the following year, and up to almost 42% for the year 1934-1935 (Annual Report, 1934-1935). The growing number of students could be explained with the hiring of new administrative support for all the divisions and with higher salaries for some administrators.

Tuition did not finance the program. Personal donations and some trust money (Hunt Fund) balanced the budget for several years. The Hunt Fund was donated securities that provided interest money to Bank Street. For instance, when facing a major balance deficit, the Board considered even selling part of the securities (Board of Trustees, 12/13/33). For instance, out of an income of $16,363.32 for the year 1932-1933 the income from tuition was $5,757.60 which represents almost a 30% in contrast to the more than 50% of income coming from "contributions" ($8,205.83). Similarly, for the year 1933-1934 out of an income of $15,754.96; only $4,568.00 came from tuition in contrast to $6,320.00 that came from "contributions," which provided about 40% more income than tuition. In the year 1934-1935 out of an income of $20,076.20; $9,233.48 came from tuition; while $8,218.03 came from "contributions." As shown in the above numbers, although the net dollar amount of contributions was higher in 1934-1935 than in previous years, the percentage that tuition provided to the budget was higher (about 30% in 1933-1934 in contrast to about 45% in 1934-1935). The increase in tuition happened because there was an increase in student enrollment. However, contributions were necessary to balance the budget (Annual Report, 1934-1935).

Student Recruitment

The recruitment strategies reveal assumptions about what type of teachers CST wanted to prepare. The type of colleges from where students were recruited assumes certain levels and domains of knowledge, liberal education, and cultural and social background.

The most usual source of new students was friends from college, family relations or progressive schools. Another important recruitment strategy was visits to women's colleges on the East Coast such as Wellesley, Vassar, Smith, Holyoke, Radcliffe, Bennington, and Barnard to speak to seniors (Annual Report, 1934-35). In addition, Bank Street organized "Open House" weekends and sent notices to college vocational directors, deans, and private progressive schools to be posted.

Another strategy used was to send letters to Deans, to Vocational Advisers, and to Heads of Departments of Education of liberal arts colleges throughout the country describing the Cooperative School and catalogs. In addition, copies of articles and paper presentations were sent to some faculty in these colleges. The only paid publicity was advertisement in the journal *Progressive Education*.

Admissions

The process of admissions also reveals the type of students that the program had in mind.

> They had an autobiography. They gave all kinds of references: college references that we could write to the people who knew them best in college, because we didn't want just a degree walking in the door. We wanted a committed, loving human being to work with children...and then they came in for other interviews within different teaching staff. Then we laid the whole thing before a committee who did the real selection.
>
> Lamb, 7/24/75, pp. 12-13.

For a concentrated and intense one-year program, Bank Street assumed that admissions had to be restricted to "...students who show promise of being able to profit fully by such an intensive program" (Outline, 1937, p. 8). Students had to provide evidence of a serious and authentic interest in teaching, of motivation to work with children, of intellectual competence, and of a "...meaningful background of social and cultural experience indicative of an alert interest in the persistent problems of contemporary society" (Outline, 1937, p. 9). The reason for not having evidence about numbers of applicants and rates of acceptance seems to be that the rate of acceptance was low, and any doubt about a student's interest or qualification could have been enough for rejection. The argument was that the education of young children was considered "too important an undertaking to permit the admission of students who because of limitations of personality or experience may become mediocre or even definitely inferior teachers" (Outline, 1937, p. 9).

Graduation from college was the basic condition that the Cooperative School established for admissions. Exceptions were made in the case of mature students with normal school background or with teaching experience. Also, there were few cases of acceptance of students whose life experiences were unique. A stated reason for such a selective process was that the program could be compared to graduate professional studies rather than the training offered in the usual normal school or teachers college. The program design and experiences assumed a lot about the students' background.

> ...It is organized to meet a different need, the need of able students already trained in the content of fundamental subject matter courses and in the methods of collecting and organizing material, who want a strictly professional year of training to fit them for teaching at the nursery and elementary school age level. In a one-year training course organized exclusively on a professional level it is imperative that students be competent to utilize such training opportunity to the full and that the School be able to presume basic content and habits of work.
>
> Outline, 1937, p. 10.

In summary, preference for admission was for college graduates, graduates of normal schools, or for mature people with expertise and experience in doing any type of art or working with children. There were no specific age restrictions, but applicants were usually rejected if they were under 21 or above 45 years. Racial or religious backgrounds were not factors in deciding upon acceptance to the program. While there was no evidence of active discrimination, there was also no evidence of active recruitment of a more heterogeneous group of students. It was expected that the student would provide at least three references, transcripts of college records, and a medical statement of a recent physical examination.

> Applicants received their confirmation of acceptance only after they have decided upon the Cooperating school in which they wish to work, and after the Director of that school has accepted the applicant. Applicants are interviewed by the Secretary or her Assistant, and by at least one other staff member before being encouraged to visit Cooperating Schools or consult directors.
>
> Obviously inappropriate applicants, or uncertain inquirers, are directed to appropriate resources for training or consultation. Applicants from great distances are seen whenever possible by some professional person known to the School, before being accepted or refused.
>
> Annual Report, 1934-1935, p. 1.

During the beginning years these interviews didn't have any objective measure of personality traits or a test of any type except the nature of the conversation with the applicant. The criteria used in these interviews were outlined as follows:

> On the positive side we are on the alert for prospective students with intellectual curiosity, some emotional insight, a profound interest in children, sustained physical and mental vitality, and awareness of social problems. We seek students who are somewhat on to themselves and the world in which they live. Students whose standards are well developed, non-crystallized and who dare try to learn for themselves. On the negative side we do not encourage applicants with severe physical handicaps, with obvious neurotic traits, including lack of humor, with foggy professional dreams, with low intellectual capacity or with a history of social and emotional rigidities and withdrawals.
>
> Annual Report, 1934-1935, p. 2.

Bank Street, by operating outside the regular institutional arrangements in which most teacher education programs existed, had the privilege of selecting who would be their students. This early selection of candidates for future teaching positions was also the result of functioning in a different market, the market of private progressive schools, which was removed from state pressures to produce large numbers of teachers at low costs.

Selection of Students

As with the controlling of number of students, the controlling of the selection process was crucial for Bank Street program quality. By selecting students who shared a similar college experience, the curriculum was structured based on the assumption of what these students would bring into the program.

Further, Bank Street did not wait for applicants. Bank Street was an active recruiter. There was a need to recruit students for teacher education programs outside the traditional sources. What Bank Street also did was to actively seek candidates in the places that were known as good liberal arts colleges assuming that their graduates had the potential to be good teachers. However, Bank Street the recruiter had to offer an attractive program that would stimulate and motivate the student beyond the exchange value of the credential. It should be an attractive option that would provide meaningful experiences, challenging content, and some sort of prestige which was not necessarily associated with teaching per se but with the people involved in the program (students, professors, schools, and communities). Bank Street illustrated this point.

However, part of this prestige can also derive from a very selective process. When the selection is demanding, it creates the sense that not everyone can have it and that only a chosen minority of people could have access to it. Furthermore, if the program proves to be meaningful and graduates are recognized as good quality, more people may want to compete for the small number of spaces in such programs. In a sense, it is like creating a new market that responds to very different criteria. Instead of easy entry, access is difficult. Instead of a set of courses with emphasis on technical knowledge, the classes respond to the already assumed good educational background of the student. In the case of Bank Street, the technical aspect is not the core of the program but is just on the periphery. Instead of thinking of the student teaching experience as a culmination, the student teaching becomes the vehicle of learning. Instead of thinking on the teaching credential as an outcome of the experiences in the program, the outcome becomes the processes of the program experiences.

If the program is not attractive to students and if its status is low, it is very difficult to recruit high quality student candidates to such program. Furthermore, if there are not many high quality student candidates, then the selectivity part of the program has no curricular impact that could build upon the high educational quality of the student.

What transpires is that while recruitment and selection are very important for the quality of the students attracted into the program, it loses its attractive powers if the program is not radically different from other teacher education programs. This difference and uniqueness not only are important for recruitment, but also sustain the aspect of student retention in the program if the program continues to be attractive and meaningful in ways that students want to stay and complete the whole program. Bank Street accomplished this retention since there are no reports of dropping out of the program or even of being counseled out. The reason for this success could be who were the people associated with the program and its content, experiences, and processes.

Size of Cohort

The size of the cohorts ranged from 25 to 30 students for each cohort in a year. The small size of each cohort of students facilitated a close relationship between faculty and students and among students themselves. The faculty knew each student. Usually, when a teacher teaches large numbers of students, it is difficult to establish close relationships. Time and energy are limited when they have to be shared by a large number of students. In contrast, having between 25 to 30 students per cohort during the course of the full program experience (course work and practice teaching), allowed the teachers at Bank Street to be closer to the students. This closeness permitted more frequent dialogue, closer attention to each student's work, more knowledge about the student throughout different experiences, and the chance for a better realization of the weaknesses and strengths of each student. This process facilitated a more individualized experience where the teacher had the possibility to engage the student in a journey of personal growth and improvement tailored for the particular needs of such student. The course on personality, taught by Healy, provided such an opportunity since personal development and learning more about the self were important aspects of becoming a teacher. The program provided a framework, but the close attention to the individual became part of the non-formal curriculum too. In a sense, this is in part what caring is about. The small size of a cohort of students provides an opportunity for faculty to care about the welfare of each student and fundamentally about the learning of each student. The small size of the group allowed the student to gain access to their teachers without difficulty.

The small size of the cohort also facilitated common group experiences. By being part of a small cohort of students, the students got to know each other throughout the program. They shared experiences, exchanged ideas, supported and challenged each other, all in a context of common objectives and purposes. An example of this was provided in the description of the field trip in the Environment course. Furthermore, the small size of the cohort facilitated the formation of a learning community, a topic that will be discussed later in this chapter.

Because of the Bank Street commitment to a close relationship and to a profound understanding of the students, they developed a new structured space in the curriculum. It was developed in the late 1930s and became formalized in the 1940s with what is nowadays known as the "advisement approach." This approach formalized the above relationships in small groups of about six students with one Bank Street faculty member. When the number of students started to grow, the advisory groups became a central part of the Bank Street curriculum. The advisory approach was a development in the Bank Street curriculum that goes beyond the scope of this work. It escapes the time framework of this study and demands in itself a careful analysis. A 1991 issue of "Thought and Practice," a contemporary journal published by Bank Street, was dedicated in its entirety to explain the "Advisement Program' approach (see also Silverman, 1970, and Feiman-Nemser, 1990).

The strudture of the program is thought provoking. First, Bank Street exemplified the potential benefits of a small cohort and a small program size. While numbers of students may be large for teacher educators, who may need to work with more than one cohort at time, for the students the cohorts offer a meaningful way of finding some community. Second, a formal space in the curriculum was created to provide a frame of reference for individualized attention when the number of students started to grow. In addition, this approach had elements of a very individualized tutoring system. While a tutoring system may not be as caring and concerned with individual needs in terms of personal dimensions, as it was in this teacher education program, it acknowledges that individuals need guided learning in a structured context. However, totally individualized learning as in tutoring was not enough for Bank Street. The small group may have provided a possibility for a smaller community within the larger community, and the opportunity to construct and interpret experiences and knowledge in a safe environment. The advantage could be the need to share experiences, testing ideas with other perspectives, and a more socially constructed learning in a structured context. Third, having more control over the number of students in a cohort allowed for a better control of the whole program. It provided a sense of the number of students who will enroll in order to plan for the different classes at different times. Control over numbers may have contributed to some control over the quality of the experience. Controlling numbers of students enrolling also meant control over who the students were.

Ownership of the Program

The Bank Street case illustrates what can happen when a set of conditions are controlled by those in charge of the program. At Bank Street the program was designed and organized by its faculty in cooperation with the schools where the practice teaching took place. This situation was unusual and permitted a direct conceptual input of the faculty into the program organization.

Ownership is an important element to foster in any teacher education program. The ways in which the program is organized, its content, its experiences, its criteria for entry and for exit, have an impact on the quality of the program. By having ownership over these components of the program, faculties also share responsibility for its quality. Moreover, ways of adjusting changes are resolved within a group of colleagues with a shared commitment. This suggests that perhaps the control of quality of a program and the control of the curriculum are to be made by its own faculty with the cooperation of practitioners. External control like that of the state does not respond necessarily to quality but to efficiency.

As mentioned previously, in the Bank Street case we find also an independence factor. The institution is not engaged in the politics of universities where competition for students and credit hours become essential for the survival of certain programs and for maintaining faculty positions. Bank Street students were the only students in the teacher education program. There were no different departments offering different courses. The value of this program resided in the experiences and the attractive and intellectually stimulating teaching it offered and not in its credentials

CHAPTER EIGHT

Bank Street and Progressive Education as Context

According to Antler (1987), Bank Street attempted to provide a synthesis among some of the contemporary progressive perspectives of the 1930s. She argues that "During the Depression, the search for a redefinition of the relationship between individuals and society brought fresh support to progressive educators who believed that the classroom could become the model for a new collectivism, integrating self-expression with larger social goals" (Antler, 1987, p. 307). As a program, Bank Street shows the blending of these perspectives in a coherent manner within the institution's curriculum and teaching of prospective teachers and in relation to the sites where student teachers practiced, with attention to a radical critique of society and with interest in child-centered practices.

Progressivisms and Teaching

Many teaching practices of progressive schools and progressive teachers during the 1930s translated mostly into what was labeled as student-centered pedagogy. Studies on child development influenced the perspective that schools should tailor the curriculum to the stages of development of the child. In the United States, G. Stanley Hall was a very influential researcher in the study of children's stages of growth and in the shaping of school curricula that attempted to meet the needs of the development of the child (Kliebard, 1995). This child-centered curriculum called for a more individualized instruction and to attend to the needs and interests of the child. These are to be properly nurtured by designing activities and materials that fit the child's stage. Certainly, a child's needs and interests are a by-product of his or her stage of development.

A different angle in progressive practices was behaviorist (Cremin, 1961/1964). The belief of these progressives was that schools can condition and change human behavior to improve human relations. Teaching in this view had to be informed by the results of research in human nature and human behavior. For instance, the curriculum in this view had to provide experiences that would prepare students to function in society and to be productive. A consequence of this perspective within progressivism was that of student selection by ability or talents, which meant to classify students to fit in determined social roles. Science could help determine the needs and capabilities of individuals, and the school could tailor a curriculum for different needs and expectations, becoming efficient as a sorting machine.

Dewey, though, (1938/1963) presented a different perspective in progressive education and advocated for active learning which starts from child interests and needs, but that happens in a learning community, in a social setting. As mentioned above, teaching should occur through educative experience, should advance expression and cultivation of individuality, free activity, understanding and engagement in a changing world, and should be relevant for the present life of students. Gordon (1988) argues that many of these views were not totally new, since European ideas about pedagogy like those influenced by Rousseau, Pestalozzi, Froebl, Tolstoy, and others, had an impact on many American educators. Educators such as Francis Parker or the same Dewey in the University of Chicago School Laboratory practiced some of these ideas in schools (for an in-depth discussion of these practices see, for instance, the edited volume by Semel and Sadovnik, 1999).

Classrooms should be environments where children live and learn to live in democratic communities. Some prefer to label this approach as community-centered curriculum and teaching (Burnett & Burnett, 1972; Hines, 1972). Schools have been conceived as places where ideas can be experimented, implemented, challenged, rethought, and reformed. In this view, the teacher creates the environment and develops a curriculum that connects subject matter with children. The teacher guides and facilitates experiences instead of being the source of all knowledge. Therefore, teachers should be knowledgeable in subject matter. This teaching is inquiry oriented with eliciting questions, with individual and group projects, and with field trips. Dewey (1903/1964) asserted that "The transition from an ordinary to a scientific attitude of mind coincides with ceasing to take certain things for granted and assuming a critical or inquiring and testing attitude" (p. 24). In this perspective, the world, the community, and life outside the school are not divorced from the classroom. On the contrary, the world is the classroom. Subject matter could be integrated through the study of themes and projects (Kilpatrick, 1918). In other words, the curriculum had flexibility, and traditional disciplines of knowledge could be taught, but there was also a need for a disciplinary base as organizational dimensions of knowledge. This type of teaching expects active learner participation. The treatment of knowledge is not static but rather explored and constructed.

This implies that the way that space and time are used abandons fixed schedules and reorganizes materials, people, and furniture with relative freedom. Management and discipline are ways of learning to live in communities. Authority is not exercised in authoritarian ways by teachers but is promoted through internalization, understanding implications of different behaviors, and by enhancing senses of respect, trust, and self-discipline.

By the 1930s several schools, mostly private, adventured into fostering this type of experiential-developmentalist community and child-centered integrated approach to teaching. Among these schools were Bank Street and its cooperating schools. However, with few exceptions, teaching in this century remained teacher-centered, with traditional exercise of authority in terms of conception of knowledge as a body of facts and procedures, and in terms of teachers and books as the only sources for such knowledge to be transmitted (Cohen, 1988, 1989; Cuban, 1993; Tyack et al., 1984). There are structural and cultural reasons that Cuban (1993) used to explain constancy in teaching practices. He also pointed out that the culture of the profession, teachers' knowledge, and teachers' beliefs and attitudes help to explain teacher-centered practices. Progressivism as an educational movement attempted to shift away from teacher-centered practices. However, progressivism was more than teaching practices.

The Progressive movement was about fostering economic, political, and social reform in the United States which began during the 1880s and lasted until about World War I (Church & Sedlak, 1976). Industry grew significantly during the past century causing several social tensions, business monopolies, city slums, marginalization, and inhumane conditions in factories and mines. During the nineteenth century the effects of industrialism were threatening the fabric of a democratic community. In spite of the accelerated economic growth, the differences between the haves and the have nots were growing. By the end of the nineteenth century, the technology derived from the uses of electricity and steam energy translated into massive production of goods. This development created a new industrial class among the owners of the means of production and an industrial underclass of workers employed in the production cycle. Artisans were displaced and many had to migrate to urban centers in search of labor (Cremin, 1988).

Urbanization increased not just with internal migration but also with massive immigration. Immigration came from East and South Europe, which was very different from prior immigration waves from Central and Western Europe. The difference was languages, but also customs, traditions, and frames of mind (Cremin, 1988). Schooling could provide an opportunity to socialize immigrants into the life, habits, conventions, and practices of a democratic community. Measures that aimed to ameliorate and revert these conditions were furthered by the progressives who demanded a greater role for the government to regulate and take responsibility in controlling social and economic relations. Progressives noticed that life conditions in cities were difficult and that the sense of shared social and political commitments were threatened if there was not an organized social intervention. Schooling provided an opportunity for human improvement (Mix, 1972). Therefore, schooling for progressives is part of a larger social reform agenda. Paraphrasing Hofstadter, Cremin asserted that the Progressive mind was, after all, that of an educator's, and often it meant to be a socially committed pedagogue. Progressives saw in schooling a mean for social and political improvement.

But progressivism did not represent one homogenous agenda. According to Westbrook (1991) to define progressivism is difficult since there are conflicting views on what progressivism means. One view argues that this movement aimed at maintaining the power and status of the old middle classes which wanted to use the state as a means to neutralize the ascending power of big industry and business, and also aimed at controlling the working-class immigrants. Another view agrees with the idea that progressivism as a movement represented middle-class interests, but rather than an old class attempting to maintain power arrangements in changing times, it was really a new technocratic and professional class with its members seeking to position themselves in power through the use of the state in the name of efficiency and expertise. However, a different perspective sees progressive reforms as a "conservative movement led by big business, rationalized by 'corporate liberal' intellectuals, and designed to create a 'political capitalism' friendly to the giant corporation" (Westbrook, 1991, p. 182).

It is not the purpose here to analyze social progressivism and educational progressivism, but rather to provide the opportunity to explore a case of progressive teacher education practices. Furthermore, it is important to clarify the generic meaning of the word *progressivism* as it is used in this context. As some scholars already argued, there are many educational progressivisms (Cremin, 1961/1964; Church & Sedlak, 1976; Kliebard, 1995). Educational progressivism was not directly connected with American Progressivism as a social movement, although both perceived democracy as a way of improving social conditions and equity (Church & Sedlak, 1976). The enormous optimism attached to industrial prosperity saw in practicality, in the power of the individual, and in scientific advances an endless source of progress. In educational terms, this meant it was necessary to search for meaningful ways in which the individual powers and capacities could be advanced with schools being the primordial institutions for the fostering of such agendas.

Cremin (1961-1964) argued that Progressivism in Education meant an effort to use schools as a way of improving the lives of individuals. In terms of curriculum it meant to broaden the scope in order to incorporate new areas such as health, vocational education, and family and community life through subjects such as Home Economics. Progressivism in Education built upon scientific research in psychology and social sciences. This also meant to address the needs of all the learners, which implies a need to better understand differences and to develop appropriate methods. Progressivism in education also was connected with: "[T]he radical faith that culture could be democratized without being vulgarized, the faith that everyone could share not only in the benefits of the new sciences but in the pursuit of the arts as well" (Cremin 1964, p. ix).

Progressive educators perceived that scientific, rational, and practical methods can help to provide opportunities to all children and youths. Within this large framework of ideas and proposals, there were different perspectives and approaches coming together or separating from each other according to the specific issues to address and to the political contingencies (Kliebard, 1995).

Some dominant perspectives within educational progressivism were influenced by Dewey's (1902, 1904, 1938) arguments on the child and the curriculum and on the role of framing educational experiences:

"Development does not mean just getting something out of the mind. It is a development of experience and into experience that is really wanted" (Dewey, 1904/1964, p. 349). Dewey (1938/1963) also argued that educative experiences lead into new educative experiences that have been framed and scrutinized to advance growth. This development and sequence of experiences, the "experiential continuum" that allow for learning, or growth in Dewey's (1938/1963) language, which is the purpose of education: "The difference between civilization and savagery, to take an example on a large scale, is found in the degree in which previous experiences have changed the objective conditions under which subsequent experiences take place" (p. 39).

According to Cremin (1961/1964), the progressive education movement developed into three distinctive and sometimes oppositional directions during the 1920s. One direction was the search for scientific answers with its center in measurement, evaluation, and efficiency, while another direction was rather experiential with some psychoanalytic influences. The third direction represented that of the radical critique. He argues that Dewey's perspectives were mostly lost through these years.

> The system of ideas that for a moment in history seemed to converge in Schools of To-Morrow and Democracy and Education fragmented; and what had appeared as minor inconsistencies in the earlier movement now loomed overwhelmingly large as different segments of the profession pushed different aspects of progressive education to their logical--if sometimes ridiculous--conclusions. Thus, Thorndike's early interest in the precise study of education blossomed into a vigorous scientism which fed on the voracious demand of the profession for esoteric knowledge that would set it apart from the layman. Similarly, Hall's early concern with child-study, now heavily overlaid with Freudianism, became a virulent sentimentalism in the hands of the Greenwich Village intelligentsia. And the reformism that had impelled Jacob Riis and Jane Addams became ever more radical in the social blueprinting of George Counts and his Social Frontier colleagues during the 1930's. (pp. 184-185)

These were also times of scientific advance and there was not just optimism, but also certainty that science would help advance social organization and justice. Dewey (1903/64) argued that science meant "A body of systematized knowledge. . . . The intellectual activities of observing, describing, comparing, inferring, experimenting, and testing, which are necessary in obtaining facts and in putting them into a coherent form" (p. 23). Scientific knowledge should inform policy, and science should be supported and accessible to all. This view of the role of science in Dewey is coherent with Westbrook's (1991) assessment that his progressive commitments should be placed together with those of Jane Addams, Randolph Bourne, and George Herbert Mead, who, as Church and Sedlak (1976) suggest, are liberal progressives who perceived community and social justice at the center of their agendas.

However, critics of the Progressive Education Association, which was founded on April 4, 1919, after the progressive movement started to decline from American politics, argue that this organization focused solely on methods and practices and did not advance social or economic ideas (Cremin, 1964). George S. Counts, in his address to the Progressive Education Association in 1932, presented a sharp critique of the movement which was entitled "Dare progressive education be progressive?" in which he spoke to the fallacies of the assumptions of neutrality of schooling, to the fallacies of child centered practices disconnected from a social context, and to the fallacies of the technocratic and efficiency views. He argued that progressive educators should educate to advance a social agenda of justice. This address, combined with two other papers, became a text: "Dare the school build a new social order?" (1932/1978). This critique of progressive educators was particularly relevant in the context of schooling in large urban settings. For example, according to Cuban (1993), in 1930 New York schools had 683 schools, 36,000 teachers, and about 1,000,000 children in one school district:

> Size alone made New York's schools unique. Yet the school district's size cannot obscure the history of tensions and compromises over ethnic, religious, political, and class issues that mirrored what was happening in other cities across the nation in the first half of the 20th century. (p. 51)

In its beginnings, the Association was on the fringes and its influence started to assert during the 1930s when the organization grew in number to about 6,000 members, and its leadership was enhanced with several prominent educators (Cremin, 1961/1964). One of the reasons for its growth was the publication of *Progressive education*, a journal founded in 1924, which by the end of the decade was a quarterly publication. Annual meetings, national committees for the study of educational problems, and the journal as an arena for debate and for dissemination of ideas, helped to promote the movement as a central space for the progressive conversation in education. Private progressive and experimental schools and teachers had an important network and central niche in the Association. Bank Street was one of these schools.

Progressive Teacher Education

The social reconstructionist perspectives that criticized a narrow view of child development and of child-centered curriculum also influenced the program at Bank Street. The critique was that the perspective of child development fostered by many progressive educators was built on a narrow psychological perspective of the individual, ignoring the social context of this individuality and ignoring the larger political and socio-economic environment (Church & Sedlak, 1976; Counts, 1932/1978; Mix, 1972; Tyack et al., 1984). Further, this critique sustained that teachers should not just understand childhood or social context but that teachers and schools should act upon the context to alter social injustice. Here, again, Dewey's perspectives are relevant since he was a friend of Lucy Sprague Mitchell, the main force behind Bank Street, and also a member of the Board of trustees at Bank Street. Westbrook (1991) argues:

> I would then place Dewey with the radical wing of progressivism ...His own alliances were formed . . .with those elements of the labor movement committed to workers' control. He flirted with socialism, but because many socialists were no more democratic than corporate liberals . . . he was wary of identifying himself with them. (p. 189)

Therefore, a community centered social agenda was crucial:

> By the eve of World War I, Dewey was more fully aware that the democratic reconstruction of American society he envisioned could not take place simply by a revolution in the classroom, that, indeed, the revolution in the classroom could not take place until the society's adults had been won over to radical democracy.
>
> Westbrook, 1991, p. 192.

This program emphasized a systematic investigation of communities and social relations as an integral part of learning how to teach. It did it, however, with a twist that enhanced the meaning to understand socio-economic and political conditions. The twist is about making it part of the subject matter to be learned and taught as an expansion of what the social studies curriculum should be about, and as an expansion of what teachers should know about the students' life experiences to be able to move them beyond these and toward new ones.

Bank Street also built strongly on Dewey's (1904) perspectives on the relationship between theory and practice. This program privileged reflective and critical experiences as sources of systematic inquiry and learning while testing consequences. In part, Dewey's ideas about the organization of practice-teaching were also present in the conceptualization and design of this aspect of the program at Bank Street. Ideas such as reflection, thoughtfulness, inquiry, constructive critique, and life-long learning, were advanced in Dewey's (1904) essay as imperative dispositions to be fostered by prospective teachers to be able to move beyond the necessary technical skills in teaching.

Moreover, another interesting variation of this program emphasized that issues of social justice not only had to be studied but had to be experienced, lived. This attitude represents a pragmatic perspective because

> As a result of their analyses, the pragmatists affirmed that thought is linked with activity; that a significant idea is in essence a plan of action, or a hypothesis, to be tested by its consequences when applied to actual existences.
>
> Childs, 1956, p. iv.

The implication of this view is that teaching should happen in an intellectually open and challenging environment that furthers systematic, scientific, inquiry, meaning that ". . . 'scientific' means regular methods of controlling the formation of judgments regarding some subject matter" (Dewey, 1903/1964, p. 24). This approach challenges also the boundaries between curriculum and pedagogy. A traditional view has been that teaching technique is separated from the subject matter. Moreover, curriculum traditionally has been perceived as the arrangement of content knowledge to be taught. However, it is suggested here that at Bank Street teaching as a subject matter of study required a specific, distinctive, pedagogy that assumed practice as part of the content to be learned. Therefore practice is part of the curriculum and not a separated and disconnected experience. Furthermore, there is no subject matter of teaching to be studied only at the intellectual level, if the act of teaching and the ideas about good teaching can't be acted, experienced, and tested. As mentioned above, this is a rather pragmatic approach since one of the fundamental principles of pragmatism rests on the possibility of testing ideas and concepts by their effects in real situations: consider Pierce's dictum that "the scientific spirit requires a man to be at all times ready to dump his whole cartload of beliefs, the moment experience is against them" (Cited in Childs, 1956, p. 284). Therefore, the content of knowledge about teaching is tested upon its real-life dimension, and, ultimately, on its effects on students' learning.

I argue that the understanding of the complexity of teaching and learning to teach, required an approach that was rather problem/issue based, contextualized and tailored, and measured by its effects. This inquiry process leads to a practical reasoning that captures what was expected at Bank Street from teachers to be able to do. For example, Barbara Biber (3/27/75), a faculty member who taught "Child Development" in the teacher education program, asserted that:

> You should understand everything you can about child development: Conscious, unconscious, developmental, Piaget, everything, but there had to be some clarity about how the teacher should act on this knowledge. That is a very difficult point, and I can't say that I can define exactly what it is. If you give me a case instance. I'll always know whether I think it's right or wrong. It's very hard to make a general theory about it.

Then, this is what practical reasoning aimed at: "give me a case instance," and with that information the teacher will evaluate alternatives, act, and again, evaluate consequences. Certainly, the judgments were also permeated by the ideological components of the beliefs about the nature of childhood, as well as about the directions of change permeated by the social reconstructionist perspective.

CHAPTER NINE

Program Impact

The Cooperative School didn't offer a state teaching certificate and didn't offer a graduate degree. Even though CST did not provide a credential valid for public schools, their credential had a high exchange value in the market of private progressive schools. Most students after one year of CST experiences were able to secure a teaching job.

Students at the CST were not motivated by a credential with exchange value in the educational market place. Rather being a graduate of the CST provided opportunities within a privileged market of private schools and educational related institutions. It was privileged not in the sense of good salaries. It was privileged in the sense of the type of student background, cultural capital, and social class of their future students, which were compatible with their own personal background. It was a desirable market for people (particularly women) with a college education and cultural capital from the middle and upper middle class because it offered them the opportunity of working with others with compatible class and social and cultural background and connections as well as with similar beliefs about education and society.

This different market for schooling required not just a different type of school and a different type of curriculum, but also required a different type of teacher. The traditional teacher education programs could not provide this type of teacher. This type of teacher for this kind of experimental schooling had to be tailored by individuals who understood these schools. CST was created for that purpose. CST, then filled a needed space in the market for teachers.

At the same time the selection had to come from a very different pool of students who had college studies and a special disposition for being lifelong learners. The prospective teachers also had to appreciate the type of cultural and social life that was valued by this self-segregated community of private progressive schools. It was not just about children and freedom, and it wasn't just about learning. The following chapter suggests that it was also about social nurturing of committed activists from a very elite class, economic, and cultural background.

The job placement report from 1934, represented in the chart below, summarizes openings listed with the job placement office at CST for that year and the number of positions filled by the CST graduates (Annual Report, 1934-1935. There is no record that establishes how many schools were listed and no data for other years for the period of this study). This chart summarizes the insertion of Bank Street graduates only in the progressive private schools market in the East Coast area. The chart, which based on data from the 1934-1935 academic year, suggests that certain places were interested in Bank Street graduates because, judging by the jobs listed, most were filled by their graduates and very few by others. It also suggests that there was a big demand for progressive teachers, particularly at the early years level, perhaps because of a growing population in progressive schools or teachers' turnover. It also suggests that most graduates secured jobs immediately (21 out of 32 students for the year 1934-1935). Without a doubt, Bank Street was filling in a vacuum as it relates to teaching vacancies in progressive schools. However, at least as it relates to the graduates of the 1934-1935 cohort, Bank Street could not satisfy alone the market need.

Figure 4: Hiring of Bank Street Graduates for 1934-1935

Position	Number of Positions	Filled by CST Students	Filled By Others
Directors	10	1	1
Teachers, ages 2 through 5	47	11	-
Teachers, ages 6 through 8	30	2	-
Teachers, ages 9 and over	23	3	1
Special subjects	40	4	2
Total	150	21	4

The relationship with the cooperating schools and other progressive schools was particularly close when it came to securing jobs. For instance, Rosemary Junior School hired four graduates from the 1931-1932 class (out of 22 students with only 19 interested in jobs). In the following three years, the same school hired five more graduates from Bank Street for teaching jobs. For the years 1931-1934, among other progressive schools in the New

York area hiring Bank Street graduates were Little Red School House, Mount Kemble School, Woodward School, Mohegan Modern School, Manumit School, Spring Hill School, and the Nursery School at Bank Street (Annual Report, 1934-1935).

Impact of the Program

The impact of this program should be considered in light of its specific expectations and context. The main purpose of the program aimed at preparing teachers who would engage in experimental, progressive, child centered, and social reconstructionist practices. The combination of a job market for graduates of the program with the positive perceptions of the alumni about the program and the positive feedback given by outsiders, suggest that the Bank Street program had a positive impact. There was a need for these types of teachers, and private progressive schools hired graduates of Bank Street based on the perception that they were exposed to a variety of experiences that furthered an open mind, to contemplate multiple perspectives, new ideas and different and new situations. The following quote captures the learning effects of the Bank Street program:

> Well, I'll tell you what Bank Street opened my eyes to: Highlander Folk School opened my eyes to all of this trouble of working people. Bank Street opened my eyes to a whole interesting world outside of books. The physical world, the environment. Lucy Sprague Mitchell's wonderful world. The relationship between environment and the life of people. Oh my, I just began to walk around New York City with brand new eyes, to see how things had grown up, why, what shape, and developed a tremendous interest in more things than in books. I owed that mainly to Lucy Sprague Mitchell.
>
> Lewis, 3/26/75, p. 61.

In the preparation of an institutional profile in 1956 that was published as a book to celebrate of the 40th anniversary of the institution since the conception of the Bureau of Educational Experiments, the Alumni Editorial Committee conducted a survey among Bank Street graduates. There were 250 questionnaires answered. In spite of some limitations of the data, I decided to use these sources because they reveal the ways in which the participants perceived themselves. There are shortcomings to these data since there is only access to the quotes that the committee published. There is no access to the instrument that gathered the information and, thus, cannot account for the validity of the survey. Another limitation is that this information does not provide the name of the person quoted, and it does not identify when the respondent attended Bank Street. However, as documented in prior chapters mainly throughout the use of the Oral Histories, the quotes below are consistent with the purposes and experiences of the CST program. The following are excerpts from the summaries created by the Committee in response to the questionnaire (Bank Street Profile: 1916-1956, 1957):

> It's good to know that there is still a whole school of people working toward a truly 'progressive' type of teaching. It gets pretty lonely out here in the educational 'wilderness' at times, and just knowing Bank Street still exists reassures me that 'it's the rest of them who are crazy not me. (p. 51)

> The delight in childhood and the recognition of children at their own levels, so inherent in Bank Street's philosophy, increased my enjoyment of my own children and my sense of wonder in their growth. (p. 52)

> The experience at Bank Street helped me to confirm my feeling that a teacher must take part in community life, that there is a unity between one's approach to little children and one's attitude to people generally. (p. 53)

> Because of Bank Street, I feel that I am better able to contribute more to children of the community-beyond my immediate environment, through various agencies. (p. 53)

In response to questions about areas of success that graduates of Bank Street faced in their own practices, alumni provided the following answers:

> Human relations, establishing rapport with children and parents, developing insights into individual problems and needs. (p. 53)

> Each child meant a great deal to me. His problems and successes were mine also. (p. 53)

> Understanding children--This is a simple statement but after teaching eight years, I have begun to realize that not many teachers really understand children. (p. 53)

> I particularly enjoyed building up the children's understanding of
> another culture from its geographical roots until they developed
> real identification with it. (p. 53)

> Planning and undertaking trips--from walks in the woods to the
> steam shovel across the street--proved to be most successful,
> meaning not only the trips themselves, but their innumerable
> values to every aspect of a first grade curriculum. (pp. 53-54)

> Setting up materials and arrangement of room, curriculum
> stimulation for intellectual curiosity, encouraging the children
> toward independence of thought and expression. (p. 54)

These areas of success are not surprising given the emphasis of the
curriculum at Bank Street on understanding children and on thinking of how
to connect children with materials and content. Further, the arrangement of
environments was studied in depth in several of the courses, in addition to
the intense and extensive practice-teaching. Moreover, it is not surprising
that they experienced success arranging field trips and teaching geography
and about different cultures since these were also dimensions of teaching and
learning that were studied in the program.

When asked about difficulties, the report showed that respondents'
answers focused on their own first years of practice. According to the report,
it seems the most frequent difficulty for graduates has been classroom
management. According to the "Bank Street Profile: 1916-1956" (1957):

> The most common single difficulty mentioned by Bank Street
> graduates as they recall their days as beginning teachers is
> discipline. Almost half the graduates who answered this question
> mention some trouble with control and with "learning to draw the
> lines and set the limits for children--learning the great variations
> between freedom and anarchy." It is extremely interesting to note
> that this percentage holds when the questionnaires are grouped by
> age level taught. Pre-school teachers have just as much trouble
> with discipline as elementary teachers. Nor does the year of
> attendance at Bank Street change this reaction. The same
> proportion of graduates of the 30s, 40s, and 50s reports concern
> with discipline. However, approximately two thirds of the alumni
> who began teaching in a public school mention difficulty with
> discipline as compared with only one half the group which began
> in a private school. (p. 54)

Difficulties with management could be explained because the program did not dedicate much time to the routines and methods of classroom life. Furthermore, coming also from a progressive child-centered perspective, these teachers were not necessarily prone to enforce authority by setting clear limits. This teaching perspective fostered the notion that limits, routines, rights, and duties have to be internalized by the children in a learning process. Thus, classroom management becomes like a unit of study in social studies since it is learning to live in community. In spite of having had classroom experience during their practice teaching, there is no evidence that student-teachers learned about discipline in the sense of controlling children's behavior. A limitation of this report is that it is not clear which year's graduates reported these difficulties. There is no evidence either about these difficulties were experienced at both private and public schools or mostly at one of these two different types of student settings. Private schools had a self-selected population of students whose parents sent them there because they chose to do so and because there was a degree of identification with the mission of the school. These were the types of schools were Bank Street students practiced during their studies and these were the schools where they taught as regular teachers in the beginning years. It would be a surprise that Bank Street graduates experienced these difficulties in private schools.

According to the summaries of the answers reported in this profile, it seems that the experience at Bank Street also had an impact beyond the professional lives of the alumni, which is consistent with the purpose of personal development (*Bank Street Profile*: 1916-1956, 1957).

> Almost half the alumni mention the influence of the Bank Street year on their personal growth, self-awareness, and maturity. More than a third commented that study at Bank Street had helped them as parents of their own children and in their community work for the welfare of all children. Many who have gone into other fields have found Bank Street teacher education an excellent foundation for other specialties such as social work, psychiatry, writing. (p. 55)

Outsiders' Perceptions

Besides the alumni reports about the impact of the program in their professional and personal lives, it is important to consider outsider perceptions. It is relevant because the program was created in cooperation with schools and practitioners. Also, it is important because of the need for a job market for Bank Street graduates. This type of feedback may influence program changes and adjustments. In an early document created by the program, there are reactions or letters written by outsiders to the Bank Street program during the early years of the program (Annual Report 1934-1935). The following quotes from letters sent by school personnel not only show appreciation for the work that Bank Street did, but they also ask for the program graduates to consider their institutions for jobs.

> I think it would be quite wonderful to secure someone from one of your Cooperative Schools. Three of my students are studying with you now and two more will enter your school next year, so you see, I have approved of your work.
> Matilda M. Remy, Director, The Anne L. Page Memorial School.

> I am enclosing some pictures of our school that may or may not help someone decide to come to Kentucky...I am swamped with applicants but I do want someone from the Bureau if that is at all possible.
> Agnes P. Sawyer, Director, Country Nursery School.

> We need a second grade teacher...I am finding difficulty in locating teachers whose fundamental approach centers around the development of the child--the kind of thing you are working out. All whom I have interviewed here are steeped in the traditional subject matter approach, being "progressive" only in methods and devices in teaching subject matter. I am attempting while building up our school and adding new members to the staff to secure the best people available.
> J. Allen Hickerson, Director, Lake Forest Day School.

> We are again looking for people and I wanted to ask you first since we would rather have someone from the Bureau than anywhere else.
> Barbara Mitchell, Director Arthur Sunshine Home.

According to the following quotes, school personnel visited Bank Street from other parts of the country. While it is not clear how they knew about the Bank Street approach to the preparation of teachers, it is clear that the program had a good reputation. Probably, by being members in the Progressive Education Association, other progressive schools knew about the nature of the Bank Street program. For instance, Winnetka schools were known as innovative and progressive, and faculty members from there visited Bank Street, too:

> It seems to me that you are doing a superb job of teaching. I have never seen more perfectly coordinated courses nor more concentrated attack upon the problem of preparing students for classroom work than I saw at your school. You were very gallant to let me in on as much of it as you did, and I am deeply grateful to you. I have come back full of ideas and new wills to succeed along various lines which were stimulated in large part by what you people are doing. Your group of students seems to be very fine and their attitude, a highly intelligent one. If that experience with you plus their own backgrounds doesn't make them good school teachers I don't believe anything could.
>
> Frances Murray, Dean, Graduate Teachers College of Winnetka.

> The short time that I was there was a real revival, rejuvenation in the atmosphere of fresh and life-giving thinking. Everything in the building, the colors and paintings done by the children, modeling, etc., spoke much. There I met a class mate of my own teacher training group--Ellen Steele. At the Cooperative School, while I was there, she led one of the best discussions I ever heard.
>
> Alice Huges, Principal, Public School in Rochester.

The comments show that Bank Street fulfilled a need in preparing progressive teachers. They also show that there was a general perception that it was effective in preparing such teachers. The active recruitment of teacher candidates by the schools represents the trust that these schools had in the positive impact of the Bank Street program on its students.

The above quotes do not say what made the Bank Street program effective. Indeed, there is no evidence in this study that the program was effective in terms of the teaching that its graduates fostered, beyond personal accounts and stories. Effectiveness is difficult to assess because there are several variables that cannot be controlled, like the places where graduates taught. To be evaluated, a program has to establish its own outcomes. Yet, how evaluation occurs, the validity of the instruments, and the interpretation of data can be very problematic. There was no formal evaluation done by Bank Street during the beginning years, which could be a result of the success that graduates experienced in the job market and the support shown by the cooperating schools.

In spite of these limitations, the set of quotes from the outsiders' letters and the comments from alumni in this chapter, and from the Oral Histories in prior chapters, provide enough information to assert that the program had a positive effect on its students. This impact has to do with personal growth, with learning about children, with learning about the world, and with learning about the classroom and school life. The examples of Lucy Sprague Mitchell's teaching in particular demonstrated how powerful the experience was in terms of learning these dimensions and in terms of advancing the conception of the teacher as an artist, as a naturalist, as a scholar and as a collaborator, as an inquirer of teaching and learning, as a researcher, and as a citizen.

Tensions: Social Background and Learning the World

Tensions mean unresolved issues, possible contradictions, conflicts, and/or unquestioned assumptions. Most students at the CST were from an elite background in terms of socio-economic background. Also, they had the experiences and knowledge that were compatible with the bohemian culture of New York in the 1930s. It is not only that they possessed the cultural capital but also the program aimed at strengthening and building upon that cultural capital. The obvious tension for these prospective teachers would be present if they had to teach children from a different background.

> Then there were quite a few plays that were coming out about the blacks and their place in society...See, we were deeply moved by the ethnic groups, but we still had not mingled with them.
>
> Killan, 2/20/76, p. 31.

Social class and privilege in terms of ethnic and social background also played a tension, like the case of what constituted the dominant perspectives of some progressive circles in relation to teaching and the personality of the teacher. For instance, different from Bank Street, expressing passion, feelings, and strong emotions were perceived in some progressive educational circles as a drawback for a teacher. These attributes in a teacher weren't desired because they might imply too much influence and too much direction in the child's learning. This was, at least, the reason given to some Jewish teachers: "She said, 'I must warn you, there is not a demand for Jewish teachers in this field.' That was true then" (Kandell, 9/15/75, p. 3). Reinforcing this perception, another student said,

> And of course the truth of the matter is, that there were in that class of forty, four Jewish students and not one of us got a job. And I don't think it was because of the College particularly. It was that at that time, in 1935, the progressive schools really believed the myth about teachers having to be serene and calm and quiet and bland, etc., etc., and that Jewish teachers were likely to be volatile and excitable and things which were not Waspish. So they either had a token Jew in a school, or they had none.
>
> Cohen, 7/7/75, pp. 4-5.

This tension was approached at Bank Street in part by the dimension of learning about the world, which also advanced the concept of active involvement in the community life, as described in prior chapters.

> I am reminded of an extremely dramatic episode in that social studies unit that I really have to tell you about. This was the year 1935-1936, and in New York City there were Nazi groups that were becoming kind of active. There was to be a big meeting of the Nazis in Madison Square Garden, and nothing would do but that incipient class of Bank Street teachers go to that meeting. If I remember correctly they also went to a Communist party meeting. At least they went to a May Day demonstration. That I know. But when the discussion arose about going to this Nazi meeting, something very interesting happened, which was that the students--I don't remember who raised this--but the question was raised, whether it was safe for the Jewish students to go. The consensus of the class was that it was better for them not to go. So we didn't go, we four. But this was openly discussed and the others went because--because you went to look at everything. This came out of social studies and was quite a special experience for me.
>
> Cohen, 7/7/75, p. 5.

Students consciously were moving away from what seems to be relatively safe into risky situations, from the known and familiar to the uncertain, from privileged class background to solidarity with the dispossessed, from assumed expectations in terms of roles because of gender or ethnicity or race to a defiance of what was deemed as normal by challenging behaviors, alliances, and social affiliations. This group of people, almost all of them women, had other choices in life. However, they crossed borders because they chose to be "educated." They chose to attend an alternative institution, to become a teacher, which was a low status profession. They chose to engage in social activism and they chose teaching as a form of changing the world. This process is messy, complex, and it is not free of tensions and contradictions. In spite of the level of awareness of those who engage in it, it is uncertain, personally challenging, and leaves many questions unanswered.

The faculty and students at Bank Street took risks because of who they were. They also had the choice of not taking any risks. However, they chose to engage in teaching and social activism and in teaching as a form of social activism. The study of how some groups lived their poverty and alienation was a subject matter of study, and it could have elicited an elitist view on how to change the lives of the poor. If this indeed was the case, it would have conveyed a patronizing approach to solve social conflicts because it was coming from those who thought that they knew better than others, the educated in contrast to the uneducated, or the empowered in contrast to the disempowered. This approach to community activism could be disempowering people in need by creating a dependency system. Westbrook (1991) noted:

> As Dewey perceived, the language of middle-class benevolence often betrayed a view of the masses as inert material on which reformers might work their will, and he called instead for a reconstructed conception of helping others which enlisted their full and willing participation in the provision of social welfare. (p. 185)

On the other hand, the Bank Street program emphasized the importance of listening to the voices of the alienated. For example, the trip to mining areas, encouraging solidarity with unions, and becoming members of these unions show an attempt to identify with the dispossessed. However, the question arises whether they were studying the lives of poor people because they wanted to teach them or because they wanted to validate their own political criticisms, or possible both. There was a profound interest in understanding children and their social context, which suggests that it was authentic. However, the available data that exists does not support that graduates of Bank Street went to teach to the mining areas with the exception of one case, Claudia Lewis, who taught for some years at the Highlander School (Lewis, 1946). This view of solving social and political problems, even with a liberal or radical candor, was consistent with their cultural capital and their social class affiliation. It fits research explanations on the education of the elite. For example, a student describes one of the schools were Bank Street student-teachers were placed as follows,

This was a school that had been organized by parents in the upper brackets of society, who had considerable wealth. They wanted their children to be educated, so that when they matured, they would be able to take on responsibilities of people who had considerable means. For example, most of the children arrived at the school driven by their chauffeurs. At the school they had hot lunch, afternoon nap--and a rather long session in the afternoon until they were picked up again. Just as an example, one child became interested in shells, so she had a little trip to Florida. Two other children became interested in Holland, so they were taken to Holland.

Killan, 2/20/76, p. 2.

The available data for these years shows that graduates of the program got jobs in private progressive schools, although, a possible reason for this phenomenon may have different roots. During the first years of the program, the teaching credential that Bank Street provided was not a valid license to teach in public schools. Furthermore, public schools were perceived as part of the problem with teaching, schooling, and social stagnation. When Lucy Sprague Mitchell and others from Bank Street, in the 1940s, started working with public schools in New York, the program gained state accreditation and graduates of Bank Street started teaching in public schools also.

Students and faculty at CST seemed to believe that what they did was authentic and that they were serious about understanding and promoting social change. However, as mentioned above, this was also a necessary component of elite education. A speculation here could be that the study of poverty and marginality, its understanding and awareness by future teachers of elite students, eventually would inform these students about the mismanagement of social issues, and about what is needed to improve the efficiency of the system, not to change it.

However, the study of marginality could be explained by another interpretation. There is reason to believe that students and faculty at Bank Street were alienated within their own social class because of their bohemian preferences and of the different lifestyles that most of them experienced.

The more I saw, the more I realized how much all this had to do with people and children... I had a wonderful roommate. Three of us got a place, Washington Square... I was so naive! One night one of the girls who'd lived in the Village before had a party. She invited many friends she knew there, and some very attractive men. I couldn't understand why these men didn't take any interest in the ladies. The girl who had lived in the Village had tons of clothes and she'd leave them dumped in the bathroom -- stockings, dresses, everything. She was working at Little Red, and she'd always stop and get a beer before she went to work.

Russel, 2/17/76, p. 2.

By opening sensitivity to different living conditions, there is a potential opening towards unconventional lifestyles and social behavior. Sensitivity in the social realm is also developed through sensitivity in the aesthetic realm. For instance, the practice and study of arts, music, and drama, is related with developing the minds and the souls towards an openness that eventually will accept differences and alternatives not just in art but also in life in general and at large. I would venture to argue that they chose to change the world through the everyday routines, through reframing themselves, and reframing their relationships. After all, it was not easy to be a woman in the 1930s, to be a social activist, and to challenge tone's own social and economic background.

This situation is full of tensions, is complex, and moves beyond large social categories and affects the formation of these student-teachers' identities, affiliations, as well as the boundaries of their social commitments and actions in teaching and in everyday life. The contributions by the Bank Street people are situated in their practice. Real situations, real dilemmas, real experiences with real children demanded a special effort to move philosophies of social change into practice. For example, one significant implication of the class on Environment was that to student-teachers learn to teach had to move away from their own comfort zones. At least in terms of teaching it meant to these student-teachers at Bank Street that they had to actively and purposefully engage in advancing an agenda of social justice through moving into the community.

CHAPTER TEN

Conclusions

"Teaching like that" at Bank Street in its beginnings during the 1930s illustrates how a progressive teacher education program was enacted and experienced. The close look at the teaching of prospective teachers helps to unpack the meaning of progressivism as experienced in this particular setting. The curriculum that Bank Street offered then had unique characteristics that were discrepant with other teacher education programs then and now. The dimensions of knowledge in learning to teach provide an interesting framework. They include learning the self, the world, the child, and the school. Bank Street had a unique relationship with the cooperating schools that enabled coherent connections. The program moved the curriculum beyond the coursework and had a focus on the student. The programmatic coherence was manifested through content, in relation to the field experiences, and in its continuity and sustainability after graduation. Having had control of the program, including recruitment and admissions, and having been outside the control of the university and the regulation of the state enabled these elements to take place.

Teaching was treated as a discipline, which means that the scrutiny of "teaching like that" created critical opportunities for students of teaching to experience, conceptualize, analyze, and evaluate consequences. The teacher as an inquirer and researcher is well supported by the examples of teaching provided in this book. Evidence has been provided about relating school and social context and making experience and teaching subject matters of study. For instance, in the courses on Environment and Language there was an emphasis on understanding how knowledge is constructed and validated. These two classes demonstrate the idea that the focus is on the student as a knower and as constructor of knowledge. Moreover, a strong connection between the ways in which the student-teachers were learning and the ways in which children learn was emphasized. A conceptual framework about structured experiences is presented: Future teachers had to experience learning and became aware of the ways in which they learned. Then, through systematic and detailed in-depth analysis, Bank Street students inquired into their own understanding in order to relate it with how children construct meaning and how they learn.

Although limited in evidence, the courses' syllabi raise interesting questions regarding the assumptions about the students in this teacher education program. There was a great deal of trust, a strong emphasis on process, products did not seem to be final, and knowledge was treated as contextualized, constructed, and temporal. Practical reasoning and pragmatic judgments seem to have served as tools in the evaluation of learning. However, the power of "teaching like that" was beyond the professional aspect of learning to teach. This process involved a unique dimension: learning about the self as a person and as a teacher. Exploring oneself started before even being accepted into the program as manifested by the recruiting practices and the admissions process that included the writing of an autobiography. Lucy Sprague Mitchell insisted that they wanted the unusual student. The Personality class, which later evolved into the "Advisory" model to support student-teachers, involved a great deal of exploration of relationships with others and about the individual dispositions and potentials. Learning about the self was connected with the other dimensions of learning to teach. For instance, the dimension of learning the world as not a social foundations class, it was much larger as it permeated learning and action, practice and reflection, in and out of the classroom contexts. This demanded an exploration, and at times a challenge of how the future teachers perceived themselves, their social and political commitments in life as much as their educational beliefs. The concern of connecting school and social context, learning about the world and the teacher as a citizen were present in what could be called an extracurricular connection. The long trip was supported with a lot of work before and after the trip, and it was supported with the commitment of many students to join the unions and with the work they were doing with the local community, whether in the tenements or after school. In a circular way, then such work was brought back to Bank Street examined what can be learn, the implications, and what the future steps for curricular development, for pedagogical approaches, and/or for social and political action might be.

Bank Street in the 1930s presented an alternative way of teaching and preparing teachers with a focus on teaching in a contextualized manner, on the process as an outcome, and on the dimensions of learning to teach. Furthermore, focusing this story mostly on an emic approach, building upon the participants' perspectives on their own experiences, enabled the reconstruction of a set of interactions, processes, and practices that provide a look behind the closed doors of classrooms, a look at the routines and meanings that constituted the positive ethos that Bank Street holds among practitioners. Therefore, by centering on meaning making rather than standards, policies, regulations, or markets, this case has provided evidence that an inquiry oriented, intellectually challenging, vibrant, and stimulating learning experience was possible in a teacher education program. However, it was necessary that faculty and students seriously engaged in making experience a subject matter of study in systematic ways and that knowledge was treated with passion and carefully examined as it connected with learners. In turn, this way of teaching had an impact on how teachers conceptualized their own practices, how they perceived their role, how they understood children and learning, how they understood themselves, and how they wanted to make the world a better place.

The pedagogy of teacher education at Bank Street contributed and was central to learning how to teach. Dialogues, conversation, critique, exploration of ideas, sharing stories, and sharing assignments were fostered in a climate of trust, caring, and intellectual respect. In turn, this opened up to a more sincere engagement without fear of being wrong or arrogant or speculative. This type of pedagogy contributed to engage in an honest intellectual climate of exploration and learning. The premise was that students of teaching should experience this type of teaching and should be aware of this teaching.

Furthermore, systematic inquiry and critical scrutiny were practiced in most experiences, and students at Bank Street became skillful in these areas as central tools for decision-making and for teaching. The development of shared ideas and concepts and ways of conveying knowledge also shaped the development of certain discourse about children and about schooling. This discourse fostered a profound intellectual respect between instructors and student-teachers and among the students. It also served as a model of the type of learning communities to be fostered in school classrooms with children. Teaching was treated as a discipline, which means that the scrutiny of "teaching like that" created critical opportunities for students of teaching to experience, conceptualize, analyze, and evaluate consequences.

I am suggesting that studying teaching as a subject matter is not modeling teaching, and it is not about showing the proper ways of teaching or reflect about it. Rather, it is to look at teaching how to inquiry or a form of research by making explicit the meanings and possibilities of the experience at hand. Certainly, this practice does not go smoothly since, at times, it means that instructors may impose on students certain activities, like these "regimes" of reflections. However, in a Tolstoyan sense (Tolstoy, 1862/1967), the teacher, who is also being taught by the students and who "walks" with the students (in yet an Aristotelian twist) still be responsible and I cannot abdicate her/his power to create situations because these situations may enhance the growth of the student. Therefore, sometimes there is a need to name resistance, confront it, and/or be directive without negotiation. Second, the teacher of teachers is sharing teaching dilemmas, tensions, conflicts, and the coping processes and solutions, including impositions, with the future teachers. This sharing goes into thinking aloud, explaining, asking questions, and brainstorming suggestions.

Treating teaching as a subject matter of study serves teachers to engage in a systematic scrutiny of practices with the cooperation or collaboration of other teachers, future teachers, and scholars in their field. This process creates an arena to validate, challenge, or even reject, discuss, exchange ideas and information, influence, and build solidarity with each other. This meant to "stop" and ask what has been happening, what was the environment like and why, what is it that they were learning and why, how different members of this "learning community" made sense of the experience and provided similar and different meaning to what seems to have been the very same experience. This also involved making overt teaching decisions, reflections, and dilemmas.

The systematic analysis and critique of teaching that is experienced firsthand, also aims at understanding the levels of uncertainty that teachers face. Not less important is to unpack the issues of power that many students many times fear to confront. Problematizing teaching provided an opportunity to discuss issues of authority, responsibility for students learning, and responsibility in building an environment to promote trust, safety, respect, and understanding of each other. This process opened a space for discussing the handling of conflict without silencing or marginalizing and to unveil meanings and consequences of the obsession with "being in charge" and "who is in charge." I am not referring here to classroom management in the sense of organization, rights and duties in a classroom, but rather, as Lucy Sprague Mitchell (1931) suggested, there is a need for awareness about your own learning or, to say this differently, there is a need to understand oneself as teachers and learners.

Likewise, this habit of inquiry by making teaching a subject matter of study means to understand that there is juxtaposition and intersection of teachers with students in relation to the subject and in relation to the experience in a social context. This forces one to look and name perceptions and the positioning of these interceptions. This is not modeling after what was experienced, but rather building on concepts and patterns identified through scrutiny of teaching and learning.

Lucy Sprague Mitchell and her colleagues at Bank Street argued that the student-teacher had to experience art, music, movement, writing, and human geography, or environment not only t learn about these disciplines, but also to become aware, to develop sensitivity, and to enhance the artistry of teaching and to understand how learning happens and how teaching facilitates or inhibits growth. They built a program and an institution that prepared a different teacher for a different school in a better and different world. This process is captured in the essence of experiencing "teaching like that."

APPENDIX

Sources and Method

In preparation for this study I explored archival material located at the Special Collections, Milbank Memorial Library, Teachers College, Columbia University, and at The Bank Street College of Education Library, New York. I used an array of sources among the archival materials in these two places, and I also used published work by the Bank Street faculty.

1. Catalogues: These contain course descriptions, requirements, and brief information about cooperating schools and about faculty interest and expertise. The main catalog used in this study is the one for the academic year 1933-1934, which does not contain page numbers.

2. Oral Histories from students, staff, and faculty: These contain transcribed interviews done during the 1970s, which were collected by Dr. Edith Gordon and her research assistants. The interviewees whom I selected were only those who were part of the program during the 1930s. Although I revised in detail all of the transcripts for this period of time, I used only sixteen of these Oral Histories because of their relevance to the focus of this investigation. This collection of Oral Histories is located under Edith Gordon Papers, at the Special Collections, Milbank Memorial Library, Teachers College, at Columbia University. Throughout this book I refer to the Oral Histories with a consistent system in order to distinguish this source from other types of documents or references. I include first the last name of the person who was interviewed. Second, I provide a short date

format consisting of the following order: (1) month, (2) day, and (3) year. If it is a quote, I also include the page number. The table at the end of this section will serve the reader to identify the background and information concerning each of the Oral Histories used, not only cited, in connection to the period studied.

3. Institutional Reports, Minutes, and Memos: The documents selected here are only those that refer to the years of this study and are mostly internal papers scattered in different files and boxes in the archives. The most useful documents of this type were the curriculum plans and outlines, in particular the one for 1937. Also, the Annual Report for 1934-1935 is very useful, but several sections have no page numbers. Minutes of the Board of Trustees meetings or of the Working Council were uneven in terms of detail. They depended a lot on the actual writer of the minutes. I hardly used these minutes as reference since many times, even when detailed, they were rather formal and they had to be taken at face value.

4. Notes from Classes: These include students' notes on class content and notes distributed in class by faculty, as well as it includes just few pieces of student work. There is not much of it in the archives.

5. Letters: There are some letters sent by or to Bank Street Schools. Usually these are addressed to faculty or Board members, and on some occasions to other institutions.

6. Published work by the faculty: It includes three issues of the bulletin "69 Bank Street" in which faculty and students published some articles in the 1930s. This bulletin had a short existence (three years) because of budget limitations. Also, Lucy Sprague Mitchell's published work is included in this category.

7. Course syllabi: There are some course syllabi. They provided some insight about the courses' content, readings, and requirements.

Figure 5: Description of Oral Histories

Name of interviewee	Date of interview	Relation to Bank Street	Year at Bank Street
Biber, Barbara	3/25; 7/21; 8/13/75	faculty	1930s
Beyer, Evelyn	9/29/78	student	1933
Cohen, Dorothy	7/7; 7/21/75	student	1935
Kandell, Florence	9/15/75	student	1935
Kerlin, Sally	7/14/75	student	1936
Killian, Aileen V.	2/20/76	student	1935
Labowitz, Margaret C.	8/8/75	student	1933
Lamb, Elizabeth	7/24/75	secretary	1930s
Lewis, Claudia	3/26/75	student	1933
Perry, Charlotte	2/14/76	student and dance inst.	1936
Rolfe, Howard & Polly	2/20/76	students	1940-1941
Russel, Virginia	2/17/76	student	1937
Schonborg, Virginia	6/11/76	student	1936
Smith, Randolph	8/25/75	faculty	1937
Tarnay, Elizabeth D.	7/8/75	student	1933
Winsor, Charlotte	2/24/75	teacher in school	1930s

This is an historical study. It involves gathering archival data and sources relevant to the time and place of the study, as well as an understanding of the time and context of the unit of analysis. As Tuchman (1994) affirms, 'Finding and assessing primary historical data is an exercise in detective work. It involves logic, intuition, persistence, and common sense" (p. 319). For this study, the unit of analysis is the teacher education program at Bank Street during the 1930s from its beginnings until the expansion of the institution into offering a teaching credential after the 1938-1939 school years. Then, Bank Street also established relationships with public schools, which then had an effect on the programs offered with more focus on practicing teachers' professional development (Sprague Mitchell, 1950). While these changes are fascinating and contribute to the understanding of the development of this institution in the 1940s and 1950s, they escape the scope of this study.

The sources of historical data for classroom and teaching description compose a puzzle with oral histories, transcripts of classroom observations, and evidence from class assignments and students work. As mentioned above, an important source of data was a set of oral histories from students, staff, and faculty, which contain transcribed interviews done during the 1970s and early 1980s. In the Spring of 1993, when researching the Bank Street Papers at the archives of the Milbank Memorial Library Special Collections I came across a set of Oral Histories. The oral histories were collected by Edith Gordon (1988) as part of her book about the history of Bank Street. The original oral histories didn't focus specifically on teacher education. Had they, my task would have been relatively straight forward. It was a big puzzle. I had to dig, to rebuild pieces, to put things together and to conceptualize how these parts go together. In the process I had to be selective, to speculate on alternatives, and to imagine or to try different arrangements and explanations. A good example of part of the process in which I engaged is described in an analogy developed by Tuchman (1994):

> Let me create this scenario: An academic department has a head clerk who has devised an idiosyncratic filing system. You have to find a form in order to receive your pay and the clerk is not available. If the form is not under "forms," maybe it's under "pay." Maybe it's under "salaries." Maybe it's under "incoming students." Maybe it's under "personnel." What categories might an idiosyncratic person have used to construct those files? ...One must discover them and check the possibilities in order of likelihood. (p. 320)

Furthermore, there are not clear descriptions of the teacher education program as a whole besides a couple of documents that summarize the curriculum. I had to put together these pieces too and reconstruct a story. Sometimes, there are missing pieces. Then, the puzzle has to be conceptualized, arranged, and put together. The process of investigating the set of archival data and the historical literature allowed me not to learn about the program, and to inquire into the experiences, expectations, conflicts, ideas, practices, and meanings of the program participants, both students and faculty.

However, the data was not nicely organized and packaged. Putting them into order was for me one of the most fun and challenging parts of this work: To imagine and test how the pieces of the puzzle and the missing pieces made sense together and fit within a larger context. Conceptualization and framing are part of the process of selecting the data and arranging the puzzle. The process is also analytical because I had to wonder why was the program this way and what was it like to be in this program in order to be able to tell the story. One more time Tuchman (1994) is helpful with her explanation: "Again, locating documents is not the end of the process... One must have both social science and historical imagination" (p. 321).

The contribution of this study is also in that it transcends the traditional sources of historical data for classroom and teaching description by composing a puzzle with oral histories, transcripts of classroom observations, and evidence from class assignments and students' work. I am mentioning all this not in order to justify my work, but rather to explain that the process was not neutral, and that in spite of the "rigor" with which I attempted to treat the data, ultimately I was responsible for filtering, selecting, and presenting. Another researcher may ask new questions and find new meanings and answers that are not approached here.

My own search for teacher education alternatives and my own concern with writing a meaningful history led me into the oral histories. I was very hesitant because these histories were not collected with a focus on the classroom experience, and I was not certain what I would encounter. My adventure with the oral histories was rewarded when by chance in one of the first oral histories I encountered, I read the one by Evelyn Beyer, who was a CSST student in 1933, who said that "This was the most exciting thing that ever happened to me: To take those courses with those women. I had never been exposed to teaching like that" (9/29/78).

This quote just inspired me to keep my search into the oral histories and other documents looking for evidence of "teaching like that."

References

Altenbaugh, R. J. & Underwood, K. (1990). The evolution of Normal Schools. In J. I. Goodland, R. Soder, & K. A. Sirotnik (Eds.), *Places where teachers are taught* (pp. 3-39). San Francisco: Jossey-Bass.

Anderson, G., & Grinberg, J. (1998). Educational administration as a disciplinary practice: Appropriating Foucault's view of power, discourse, and method. *Educational Administration Quarterly*, 34 (3), 329-353.

Antler, J. (1982). Progressive education and the scientific study of the child: An analysis of the Bureau of Educational Experiments. *Teachers College Record*, 83(4), 559-591.

Antler, J. (1987). *Lucy Sprague Mitchell: The making of a modern women.* New Haven, CT: Yale University Press.

Annual Report (1934-1935). Unpublished manuscript. Bank Street College of Education Library, New York.

Ayers, W. (1988). A teacher's life more fully lived. *Teachers College Record*, 89(4), 579-586.

Bank Street Profile, 1916-1956 (1957). New York: Bank Street College of Education.

Black, I., & Blos, J. (1961). *L. S. Mitchell as a--.* Unpublished manuscript. Bank Street Archives, Special Collections, Milbank Memorial Library, Teachers College, Columbia University, New York.

Bonner, F. G. (1929). The training of teachers for the new education. *Progressive Education*, 6, 111-121.

Bourdieu, P. & Passeron, J. (1977). *Reproduction in education, society, and culture.* London: Sage Publications.

Bowman, E. (1935). *Unpublished memo.* Bank Street Archives, Special Collections, Milbank Memorial Library, Teachers College, Columbia University, New York.

Burnett, J. H. & Burnett, J. R. (1972). Issues in school-community relations in the present period. In J. R. Squire (Ed.), *A new look at progressive education* (pp. 118-165). Washington, DC: Association for Supervision and Curriculum Development.

Catalog (1933-1934). Unpublished document. Bank Street College of Education Library, New York.

Childs, J. (1956). *American pragmatism and education.* New York: Holt.

Church, R. L. & Sedlak, M. W. (1976). *Education in the United States: An interpretive history.* New York: The Free Press.

Clifford, G. (1980). Distortion of the historiography of American education: The problem of silence. In H. D. Gideonse, R. Koff, & J. J. Schwab (Eds.), *Values, inquiry, and education* (pp. 139-158). UCLA: Center for the Study of Evaluation.

Clifford, G., & Guthrie, J.W. (1988). *Ed school: A brief for professional education.* Chicago: University of Chicago Press.

Cohen, D. K. (1988). *Teaching practice: Plus ca change....* National Center for Research on Teacher Education, Michigan State University, East Lansing, MI.

Cohen, D. K. (1989). Practice and policy: Notes on the history of instruction. In D. Warren (Ed.), *American teachers: Histories of a profession at work* (pp. 213-236). New York: Macmillan.

Counts, G. S. (1932/1978). *Dare the school build a new social order?* Carbondale: Southern Illinois University Press.

Course outline (1936-1937). Unpublished document. Bank Street Archives, Special Collections, Milbank Memorial Library, Teachers College, Columbia University, New York.

Cremin, L. A. (1961/1964). *The transformation of the school: Progressivism in American education, 1876-1957.* New York: Knoff.

Cremin, L. A. (1988). *American education: The metropolitan experience 1876-1980.* New York: Harper & Row.

Cuban, L. (1993). *How teachers taught: Constancy and change in American classrooms 1880-1990 (2nd ed.).* New York: Teachers College Press.

Curriculum plans (1934-1935). Unpublished document. Bank Street Archives, Special Collections, Milbank Memorial Library, Teachers College, Columbia University, New York.

Dewey, J. (1902/1964). The child and the curriculum. In R. D. Archambault (Ed.), *John Dewey on education: Selected writings* (pp. 339-358). Chicago: University of Chicago Press.

Dewey, J. (1903/1964). The relation of science and philosophy as a basis for education. In R. D. Archambault (Ed.), *John Dewey on education: Selected writings* (pp. 295-310). Chicago: University of Chicago Press.

Dewey, J. (1904/1964). The relation of theory to practice in education. In R. D. Archambault (Ed.), *John Dewey on education: Selected writings* (pp. 313-338). Chicago: University of Chicago Press.

Dewey, J. (1933/1964). Why reflective thinking must be an educational aim. In R. D. Archambault (Ed.), *John Dewey on education: Selected writings* (pp. 212-228). Chicago: University of Chicago Press.

Dewey, J. (1938/1963). *Experience and education.* New York: Macmillan.

Editorial (1931). *Progressive Education*, 8, 280-281.

Feiman-Nemser, S. (1990). Teacher preparation: Structural and conceptual alternatives. In W. R. Houston (Ed.), *Handbook of research on teacher education* (pp. 121-33). New York: Macmillan.

Feiman-Nemser, S. and Floden, R. (1986). The cultures of teaching. In M. C. Wittrock (Ed.), *Handbook of research on teaching* (pp. 505-526). New York: Macmillan.

Finkelstein, B. (1992). Education historians as mythmakers. In C. Grant (Ed.), *Review of research in education*, 18 (255-297). Washington, DC: AERA.

Foucault, M. (1981). *Power/knowledge: Selected interviews and other writings, 1972-1977* (Colin Gordon, Ed.). New York: Random House.

Foucault, M. (1990). *Politics, philosophy, culture: Interviews and other writings, 1977-1984* (Lawrence Kritzman, Ed.). London: Routledge.

Ginsburg, M. (1988). *Contradictions in teacher education and society.* New York: The Falmer Press.

Goodlad, J. I., Soder, R., & Sirotnik, K. A. (Eds.). (1990). *Places where teachers are taught.* San Francisco: Jossey-Bass.

Gordon, E. L. (1988). *Education the whole child: Progressive education and Bank Street college of education, 1916-1966.* Unpublished doctoral dissertation, State University of New York, Stony York Brook.

Gore, J. (1993). *The struggle for pedagogies: Critical and feminist discourses as regimes of truth.* New York: Routledge.

Grinberg, J. (2001). Clase y género: el caso de las mujeres docentes en el Bank Street (Class and gender: The case of the women practitioners at Bank Street). In *Electronic Memory of the First International Conference on Processes of Feminization of Teacher Education.* Mexico: El Colegio de San Luis de Potosi (ISBN 968-7727-58-6).

Grinberg, J. (2002). "I had never been exposed to teaching like that": Progressive teacher education at Bank Street during the 1930's. *Teachers College Record*, 104 (7), 1422-1460.

Grinberg, J., & Goldfarb, K. (1998). Moving teacher education in/to the community. *Theory Into Practice*, 37 (2), 131-139.

Grinberg, J., & Saavedra, E. (2000). The Constitution of Bilingual/ESL Education as a Disciplinary Practice: Genealogical Explorations. *Review of Educational Research*, 70 (4), 419-441.

Herbst, J. (1989). *And sadly teach: Teacher education and professionalization in American culture.* Madison: University of Wisconsin Press.

Hines, V. A. (1972). Progressivism in practice. In J. R. Squire (Ed.), *A new look at progressive education* (pp. 118-165). Washington, DC: Association for Supervision and Curriculum Development.

Jackson, P. (1986). The mimetic and the transformative. In *The practice of teaching*, (115-145). New York: Teachers College Press.

Jervis, & Montag, (1991). *Progressive education for the 90's.* New York: Teachers College Press.

Kilpatrick, W. H. (1918). The project method. *Teachers College Record*, 19, 319-35.

Kincheloe, J. (2002). *Teachers as Researchers: Qualitative Inquiry as a Path to Empowerment (2nd. Edition)*. New York: Routledge.

Kincheloe, J. (2004). *Critical pedagogy: A primer*. New York: Peter Lang.

Kliebard, H. M. (1995). *The srtuggle for the American Curriculum: 1893-1958 (2nd. edition)*. New York: Routledge.

Labaree, D. F. (1992). Power, knowledge, and the rationalization of teaching: A genealogy of the movement to professionalize teaching. *Harvard Educational Review, 62*, 123-154.

Labaree, D. F. (1994). An unlovely legacy: The disabling impact of the market on American teacher education. *Phi Delta Kappan, 75* (8), 591-5.

Lewis, C. (1946). *Children of the Cumberland*. New York: Columbia University Press.

Liston, D., & Zeichner, K. (1990). *Teacher education and the social conditions of schooling*. New York: Routledge.

Minutes of the Board of Trustees Meetings (1933, 1934). Unpublished documents. Bank Street Archives, Special Collections, Milbank Memorial Library, Teachers College, Columbia University.

Mix, M. D. (1972). Social constructionism, past and present. In J. R. Squire (Ed.), *A new look at progressive education* (pp. 118-165). Washington, DC: Association for Supervision and Curriculum Development.

Minutes of the Board of Trustees Meetings (1933, 1934). Unpublished documents. Bank Street Archives, Special Collections, Milbank Memorial Library, Teachers College, Columbia University, New York.

Ms Mitchell's class in Language (1931). Unpublished transcript. Bank Street Archives, Special Collections, Milbank Memorial Library, Teachers College, Columbia University, New York.

Outline of a teacher education curriculum (1937). Unpublished document. Bank Street Archives, Special Collections, Milbank Memorial Library, Teachers College, Columbia University, New York.

Perrone, V. (1989). *Working papers: Reflections on teachers, schools, and communities*. New York: Teachers College Press.

Popkewitz, T. (Ed.) (1987). *Critical studies in teacher education: Its folklore, theory and practice*. New York: Falmer.

Rury, J. L. (1989). Who became teachers? The social characteristics of teachers in American history. In D. Warren (Ed.), *American teachers: Histories of a profession at work* (pp. 9-48). New York: Macmillan.

Rutkoff, P. M. & Scott, W. B. (1986). *New school: A history of the new school for social research*. New York: Free Press.

Sadovnik, A., & Semel, S. (2002). *Founding mothers and others: Women educational leaders during the Progrssive era*. New York: Macmillan.

Schwab, J. J. (1976). Education and the state: Learning community. In *Great ideas of today* (pp. 234-271). Chicago: Encyclopedia Britannica.

Segall, A. (2002). *Disturbing practice*. New York: Peter Lang.

Semel, S., & Sadovnik, A. (1999). *"Schools of tomorrow" schools of today: What happened to Progressive education*. New York: Peter Lang.

Silverman, C. (1970). *Crisis in the school*. New York: Random House.

Splitter, L., & Sharp, A. (1995). *Teaching for better thinking: The classroom community of inquiry*. Australia: Australian Council for Educational Research.

Sprague Mitchell, L. (1931). A cooperative school for student teachers. *Progressive Education*, 8, 251-255.

Sprague Mitchell, L. (1950). *Our children and our schools*. New York: Simon and Schuster.

Steinberg, S., & Kincheloe, J. (Eds.) (1998). *Students as researchers: Creating classrooms that matter*. New York: Falmer Press.

Students' memo (no date*)*. Bank Street Archives, Special Collections, Milbank Memorial Library, Teachers College, Columbia University, New York.

Syllabi (1936-1937*)*. Unpublished documents. Bank Street Archives, Special Collections, Milbank Memorial Library, Teachers College, Columbia University, New York.

Teacher Education Curriculum (1938). Unpublished document. Bank Street Archives, Special Collections, Milbank Memorial Library, Teachers College, Columbia University, New York.

The students of the cooperative school, 1934-1935 (1935). No title. *69 Bank Street,* 1 (8), 1-2. Bank Street College of Education Library, New York.

Tolstoy, L. (1862/1967). Are the peasant children to learn to write from us? Or, are we to learn from the peasant children? In *Tolstoy on Education*, edited by R. Archambault (191-224). Chicago: The University of Chicago Press.

Tuchman, G. (1994). Historical social science: Methodologies, methods, and meanings. In N. K. Denzin, & Y. S. Lincoln (Eds.), *Handbook of qualitative research* (pp. 306-323). Thousand Oaks: Sage.

Tyack, D., Lowe, R., & Hansot, E. (1984). *Public schools in hard times: The great depression and recent years*. Cambridge: Harvard University Press.

Urban, W. J. (1990). Historical studies of teacher education. In W. R. Houston (Ed.), *Handbook of research on teacher education* (pp. 59-82). New York: Macmillan.

Warren, D. (1985). Learning from experience: History and teacher education. *Educational Researcher*, 14(10), 5-12.

Warren, D. (Ed.) (1989). *American teachers: Histories of a profession at work*. New York: Macmillan.

Westbrook, R. B. (1991). *John Dewey and American democracy*. Ithaca: Cornell University Press.

Winsor, C. B. (1973). *Experimental schools revisited: Bulletins of the Bureau of Educational Experiments*. New York: Agathon Press.

Zeichner, K., and Gore, J. (1990). Teacher socialization. In W. R. Houston (Ed.), *Handbook of research on teacher education* (pp. 329-348). New York: Macmillan.

Zeichner, K. (2003). The adequacies and inadequacies of three current strategies to recruit, prepare, and retain the best teachers for all students. *Teachers College Record,* 105 (3), 490-519.

Oral Histories

Beyer, E. (9/29/78). Oral Histories, Edith Gordon Papers, Bank Street Archives, Special Collections, Milbank Memorial Library, Teachers College, Columbia University, New York.

Biber, B. (3/25, 7/21, 8/13/75). Oral Histories, Edith Gordon Papers, Bank Street Archives, Special Collections, Milbank Memorial Library, Teachers College, Columbia University, New York.

Cohen, D. (7/7, 7/21/75). Oral Histories, Edith Gordon Papers, Bank Street Archives, Special Collections, Milbank Memorial Library, Teachers College, Columbia University, New York.

Kandell, F. (9/15/75). Oral Histories, Edith Gordon Papers, Bank Street Archives, Special Collections, Milbank Memorial Library, Teachers College, Columbia University, New York.

Kerlin, S. (7/14/75). Oral Histories, Edith Gordon Papers, Bank Street Archives, Special Collections, Milbank Memorial Library, Teachers College, Columbia University, New York.

Killan, A. V. (2/20/76). Oral Histories, Edith Gordon Papers, Bank Street Archives, Special Collections, Milbank Memorial Library, Teachers College, Columbia University, New York.

Labowitz, M. C. (8/8/75). Oral Histories, Edith Gordon Papers, Bank Street Archives, Special Collections, Milbank Memorial Library, Teachers College, Columbia University, New York.

Lewis, C. (3/26/75). Oral Histories, Edith Gordon Papers, Bank Street Archives, Special Collections, Milbank Memorial Library, Teachers College, Columbia University, New York.

Russel, V. (2/17/76). Oral Histories, Edith Gordon Papers, Bank Street Archives, Special Collections, Milbank Memorial Library, Teachers College, Columbia University, New York.

Schonborg, V. (6/11/76). Oral Histories, Edith Gordon Papers, Bank Street Archives, Special Collections, Milbank Memorial Library, Teachers College, Columbia University, New York.

Smith, R. (8/25/75). Oral Histories, Edith Gordon Papers, Bank Street Archives, Special Collections, Milbank Memorial Library, Teachers College, Columbia University, New York.

Tarnay, E. D. (7/8/75). Oral Histories, Edith Gordon Papers, Bank Street Archives, Special Collections, Milbank Memorial Library, Teachers College, Columbia University, New York.

Winsor, C. (2/24/75). Oral Histories, Edith Gordon Papers, Bank Street Archives, Special Collections, Milbank Memorial Library, Teachers College, Columbia University, New York.

Studies in the Postmodern Theory of Education

General Editors
Joe L. Kincheloe & Shirley R. Steinberg

Counterpoints publishes the most compelling and imaginative books being written in education today. Grounded on the theoretical advances in criticalism, feminism, and postmodernism in the last two decades of the twentieth century, Counterpoints engages the meaning of these innovations in various forms of educational expression. Committed to the proposition that theoretical literature should be accessible to a variety of audiences, the series insists that its authors avoid esoteric and jargonistic languages that transform educational scholarship into an elite discourse for the initiated. Scholarly work matters only to the degree it affects consciousness and practice at multiple sites. Counterpoints' editorial policy is based on these principles and the ability of scholars to break new ground, to open new conversations, to go where educators have never gone before.

For additional information about this series or for the submission of manuscripts, please contact:

Joe L. Kincheloe & Shirley R. Steinberg
c/o Peter Lang Publishing, Inc.
275 Seventh Avenue, 28th floor
New York, New York 10001

To order other books in this series, please contact our Customer Service Department:

(800) 770-LANG (within the U.S.)
(212) 647-7706 (outside the U.S.)
(212) 647-7707 FAX

Or browse online by series:
www.peterlangusa.com